Hokus Pokus

A Practical Guide To Deconstruction

By Francis Marion

The picture of *Plato's Allegory of the Cave* on the front cover is a visual image that reflects the contents of this book. There are prisoners in a cave who are chained to a wall, staring at shadows since childhood, believing the shadows are real.

Dedication

This book is dedicated to the modern-day prophets who are speaking truth and wisdom to the prisoners in the "cave."

Contents

Socrates said,

"I cannot teach anybody anything.

I can only make them think."

Preface

I want to warn the reader that some of the content in Hokus Pokus may be disturbing. It is not intended to attack anyone's religious beliefs or pass judgment. The content of this book goes far beyond the typical discussion about deconstructing one's faith and answers the BIG questions. The contents of Hokus Pokus challenge a person to use deconstruction as a steppingstone towards spiritual awakening.

Hokus Pokus looks at the big picture. There is an ancient parable about six blind men and an elephant that teaches a profound lesson.

The tale goes like this. An elephant was brought into a town, and there were six blind men who could not see it. They were all curious about the elephant and decided to inspect it by touching it. The first blind man touched the trunk of the elephant and thought it was a thick snake. The second blind man touched the elephant's ear and thought it was a big fan. The third blind man touched the elephant's leg and thought it felt like a tree trunk. The fourth blind man touched the side of the elephant and told the others, "It is a wall." The fifth blind man touched the tail of the elephant and described it as a rope. The sixth and last blind man felt the ivory tusk and told the others in the group that the elephant was hard and smooth, so it had to be a spear.

The moral of this tale implies that one's subjective perception is limited because of insufficient knowledge. Deconstruction is much more than just looking at the "tail of the elephant" or the "trunk of the elephant" to reach a definitive conclusion about one's faith.

Hokus Pokus gives the reader knowledge and insights that help one see the big picture or the "whole elephant." When the reader sees the "whole elephant" for the first time, it will be very disturbing. This will be like Dorothy in the Wizard of Oz discovering the truth about the Wizard. He was a fraud, hoaxster, and a deceiver. She yelled at him… "I don't believe you!"

The beginning of the book talks about non-threatening topics like spiritual gaslighting, fearmongering, and spiritual bondage. It continues with Plato's Allegory of the Cave, The Wizard of Oz, Fairy Tales, and Hollywood movies that illustrate spiritual awakening outside of traditional religion.

The water gets deeper when the book goes into the "hokus pokus" of man-made religion. The next section looks at the early church history and the genocide of Christian "heretics" by the Catholic Church during the Middle Ages. All this information is important because the content builds on top of each chapter. It is like climbing a ladder and when one gets to the top, the reader will see (spoiler alert) a wolf in sheep's clothing. Hokus Pokus is filled with disturbing content that uncovers the truth that has been covered up by man-made religion.

The last chapter is mind-blowing and quite disturbing because it talks about the thousands of evil-looking gargoyles roosting on churches and cathedrals throughout Europe. The Cathedral of Notre Dame in Paris has 102 gargoyles roosting on it. Hokus Pokus explains why these evil creatures are looking down on people in the cities.

Finally, the book pulls back the curtain and reveals the invisible rulers who are written about in the Bible and ancient texts. These are the evil powers and principalities who rule over the world. They influence your thoughts, emotions, and actions. These forces of darkness have infiltrated all aspects of our lives, creating chaos, confusion, fear, and evil. The reader will learn how these evil tricksters use a counterfeit spirit to change good into evil, and light into darkness.

Although this book is disturbing, it is also empowering because it encourages the reader to recognize the "shadows" are not real. The picture on the front cover is a visual image of Plato's Allegory of the Cave that reflects the overall contents of this book. There are prisoners in a cave staring at shadows since childhood believing the shadows are real.

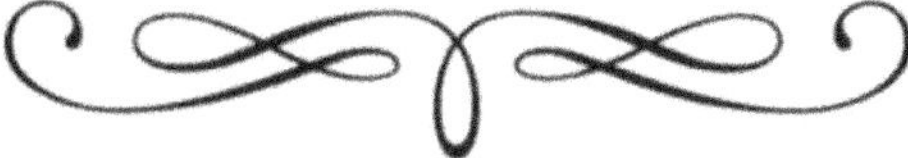

People often ask me what religion are you, or what church do you go to. I tell them that I belong to the Church of None and it is the fastest growing religion in the country. I usually get a blank stare before I hear, "never heard of it."

I joined the Church of None about 20 years ago when my pastor suggested that I find another church. At the time, I was on the church board, taught Sunday School, and even was asked to fill in on a Sunday or Wednesday night service to give a teaching.

As I was preparing for my lessons, a silent voice inside me spoke to my spirit that something is not right, and I needed to rethink everything that I was taught as a child and later as an adult. I put on my "critical thinking" glasses and started to read and study material that challenged my core beliefs. Because everything that I read made a lot of sense, I was challenged to keep searching for answers. It did not take very long to see the hokus pokus that my church was teaching.

One day I went to my pastor and shared some of the things that I was learning. He could not respond with a meaningful answer to my questions and concerns. Our meeting ended when he said that it would be better if I found another church. This was one of the best things that ever happened to me. That is when I joined the Church of None. The "Nones" account for nearly 30% of the U.S. population. The term "none" is a label given to those who are unaffiliated with organized religion.

My Church of None has "none" of this…. No religious hokus pokus, no dogmas and creeds, no church buildings, no fear, no guilt, no condemnation, no hell, no judgment, and no delusional thinking. My Church of None is about a relationship with the True God. It honors critical thinking and asking questions.

I have the freedom to interpret scripture as allegories, metaphors, and parables and permission to read all the "banned and heretical" texts, like the Gnostic Gospels, which do not agree with the teachings of man-made religion. The Church of None is universal and not inclusive. There is no hierarchy to tell me what I must believe. I am free to read, study, and listen to spiritual teachers that I choose. It is not a religion but a personal experience.

Hokus Pokus is a thought-provoking and insightful book that strips away the delusional thinking and hokus pokus that keeps individuals in bondage to man-made religion. It will challenge you, disturb you, and make you think. I hope that this book helps you escape from the "cave."

Thank you for reading this.

Best wishes on your journey along the "yellow brick road."

Francis Marion

Illusion and Delusion

Illusion

Magic shows are one of the most popular attractions in Las Vegas. David Copperfield, Chris Angel, Shin Lim, Matt Franco, and Penn & Teller are just a few of the most recognizable names performing their magic in magnificent showrooms. People pay top dollar for tickets; their performances are usually sold out. What is the big draw that attracts so many people to magic shows? Can you relate to the disbelief and awe everyone in the audience experiences?

Many people vividly remember an "illusion" they witnessed at a magic show. I recall a dinner show at the Dixie Land Stampede in Branson, Missouri. There were beautiful horses, trick riders, clowns, and a lot of entertaining things to watch. But I still cannot forget the two covered wagons racing to the far end of the arena. At the back of one of the wagons, a young girl waved at the crowd. She ducked into the wagon and disappeared. A few seconds later when the race was over, the same young lady appeared in the back of the second covered wagon waving at the crowd. How did she do this? I have seen this performance several times and it still is an amazing illusion.

One can go on YouTube and watch David Copperfield walk

through the Great Wall of China or make the Statue of Liberty vanish. There are videos showing people and elephants disappearing or a giant saw that slices a person into two parts. People love to watch the illusion even though they know it is not real.

The words "illusion" and "delusion" often express similar ideas. Although many believe these words mean the same thing, they are radically different. Illusion comes from the Latin word "eluder," meaning "to mock." Illusions trick or mock our brains into perceiving something that is not real. Optical illusions are often used as mind games or puzzles to entertain people.

Magic has been around for centuries as an art form where a magician fools people using all sorts of illusionary tricks. They make things appear and disappear. With a sleight of hand or hokus pokus, abracadabra, the magician mocks one's brain into believing something unreal. An illusion is based on optical or sensory perception. It takes our focus away from the main objective by using sensory images that mislead the brain into thinking that false perception is the true reality. Optical illusions fascinate people because they amaze us when we discover that our brain fooled us into seeing something that is not real.

This image will "mock" your brain into seeing something unreal. **<u>Stare at the four dots in the center of the image for thirty seconds. Next, look at a blank wall and start blinking your eyes.</u>** Who do you see? Did your brain fool you into seeing a shadow or image of Jesus that was not there? The surprise of seeing a picture of Jesus on the wall is surreal. You certainly know that the image is just an optical illusion. Your personal experience of seeing an illusionary picture on the wall will have a deeper meaning when the book talks about the "shadows" on the wall of Plato's cave.

If you keep reading this book, you will learn about the ultimate mind-blowing illusion that has been mocking your brain and tricking you into seeing something that is not real. It is the greatest illusion ever created because it makes the universe disappear.

Delusion

The Latin word for delusion is "delusionem" which means deceiving. Unlike an "illusion" that receives false information from the senses, a delusion, such as a lie, receives false cognitive information and believes it to be true. A delusion is a false belief resistant to confrontation and will not change despite evidence to the contrary. It is much more serious because it controls a person's ability to make rational decisions and forces one to believe in something that is not true or real.

When the brain receives false and misleading information, such as lies, and other distortions of the truth, it deciphers the data as either true or false depending on the preconceived mental state of the individual. Often a delusional person will receive false information and interpret it as confirmation and reinforcement that supports their erroneous perception of the truth. The Cambridge Dictionary defines delusion as "something a person believes and wants to be true when it is not." Your brain creates your perception of the world. This means that your brain fills in gaps when there is incomplete information. In a delusion, the brain creates a false image or belief. Individuals trapped in a delusion are prone to believing errors and lies and see them as truth. A delusion is like a mental fortress that resists both common sense and overwhelming evidence to the contrary.

Studies reveal the existence of an illusory truth effect that occurs when false information is repeated over time. Individuals most often believe something is true because they heard it many times in the past. The foundational principle of the illusory truth effect suggests repetition makes a false idea much easier to believe. Billions of people believe hokus pokus is true because it has been repeated for hundreds of years. Repeating delusional thinking and false information does not change hokus pokus into truth. "The illusory truth effect, also known as the illusion of truth, describes how, when we hear the same false information repeated again and again, we often come to believe it is true. Troublingly, this even happens when people should know better-that is when people initially know that the misinformation is false." (The Decision Lab, Why do we believe misinformation more easily when it's repeated many times?)

Delusional thinking will be explained later in the book as a counterfeit spirit that deceives and tricks the mind.

What Do You See?

An old lady or a young lady? A rabbit or a duck?

The literal story or the hidden symbolism

Illusion and Delusion

We can read numerous passages in the Bible that warn individuals about a strong delusion. The premise of this book is to demonstrate that this "strong delusion" has blinded millions or billions of people in the world over the centuries into believing a lie. They are like the "shadows" in Plato's cave. Although the Bible warns us about a "strong delusion," most people will dismiss this and think it refers to someone else or another religious group.

"Denial is the most predictable of all human responses."

(The Architect, Matrix Reloaded)

Mystics throughout the ages have used coded language to communicate their esoteric wisdom. They disguised their message in common words like cave, mountain, water, air, earth, man, woman, etc., to fool those on the outside. They also used numbers and names to hide and protect their teachings about the sacred mysteries. In the New Testament, Jesus used the same approach to teach his disciples about the Kingdom of Heaven when he spoke in parables. This literary technique has "blinded" unawakened souls into believing hokus pokus.

Hokus Pokus
A Practical Guide to Deconstruction

Hiding the esoteric and symbolic message in a literal story resonates with the words of Jesus of Nazareth… "Therefore speak I to them in parables, because seeing, they see not, and hearing, they hear not, neither do they understand." (Matt 13:15)

Plato's Allegory in The Cave uses prisoners chained to a wall to illustrate how mankind has been fooled and deceived by "shadows" that are not real. The remainder of this book will use fairy tales, the Wizard of Oz, Hollywood movies, and the Christian Bible to reveal the universal message that transcends the delusional thinking and hokus pokus of man-made religion.

Deconstruction and Occam's Razor

Searching for your inner truth may feel like you are lost in a maze. There are so many opinions and ideas to sort out. One can feel overwhelmed and inadequate to figure things out. The only thing that you know for sure is that your intuition is telling you something is not right with your religious beliefs.

Occam's Razor is a philosophical principle that dates to the fourteenth century. This brilliant rule for solving a difficult problem is associated with William of Occam who lived between 1285-1348. He was an English theologian and Franciscan friar. The true origin of Occam's Razor is still debatable as many scholars believe it goes back to ancient times.

The main idea behind Occam's Razor follows the footsteps of modern detectives, medical doctors, scientists, and others searching for answers to difficult questions. A doctor must consider all the symptoms before he can give a diagnosis and a detective must check out all the clues before he links someone to a crime. Occam simplified the problem-solving dilemma by suggesting the truth is simple and not complicated. ….

The simplest answer is most often correct.

Occam used the visual imagery of a razor to communicate the cutting away or shaving away all the unnecessary or unlikely explanations. A jackhammer is more realistic for someone who is deconstructing. It may take a jack hammer to bust through the layers of hokus pokus and years of indoctrination. One can look at deconstruction as the shaving away of delusional thinking, myths, and false evidence appearing real.

Jefferson's Bible

Thomas Jefferson took a razor and physically removed the "hokus pokus" from his Bible. Many religious writers and right-wing fundamentalists did a hokus pokus on Thomas Jefferson and many of the other founding fathers by reinventing them to look like orthodox Christians. The former president was a deep spiritual thinker who dismissed the Trinity, virgin birth, the miracles of Jesus, and the resurrection. Jefferson believed Jesus of Nazareth was a holy man and a preeminent teacher. More importantly, he rejected the divinity of Jesus of Nazareth.

Using his razor, he cut and pasted the text into a scrapbook that he bound in red leather. "The ex-president bent over the book, using a razor and scissors to carefully cut out small squares of text." (History Channel, Why Thomas Jefferson Rewrote the Bible Without Jesus' Miracles and Resurrection, August 1, 2019) This is commonly known as the Jefferson Bible. He wrote two volumes, The Philosophy of Jesus of Nazareth and the Life and Morals of Jesus of Nazareth. Jefferson's Bible is condensed into eighty-four pages. This national treasure is on display at the Smithsonian Museum. One can also purchase a copy online.

Thomas Paine

Thomas Paine was a founding father, political activist, philosopher, and a truth seeker. He had a profound influence on molding the independent spirit of the colonists and the shaping of the Declaration of Independence. He wrote a short pamphlet called Common Sense that sold more than 500,000 copies that inspired the American Revolution.

He also wrote another pamphlet, The Age of Reason, which sparked a revival in religious "deconstruction" and free thinking. Paine was a deist who believed in the True God but rejected the divinity of Jesus. He belonged to a brotherhood of other colonial Deists who included George Washington, Thomas Jefferson, Benjamin Franklin, James Madison, and James Monroe, and others.

Deconstruction and Occam's Razor

Because Thomas Paine attacked organized religion, his thought-provoking ideas were ridiculed and rejected by Christians. Although schools across America "banned" Paine's "heretical" book, it still stands out today as a popular resource for truth seekers. The ideas of Thomas Paine are more relevant today as individuals search for meaningful information that exposes the hokus pokus of organized religion.

Trying to summarize The Age of Reason would be an injustice to the book and to the courage of Thomas Paine for expressing his views to a closed-minded and hostile audience. Here are several quotes from Thomas Paine's book.

"It is the duty of every man, as far as his ability extends, to detect and expose delusion and error. But nature has not given to everyone a talent for that purpose, and among those to whom such a talent is given, there is often a want of disposition or of courage to do it." Thomas Paine, <u>The Age of Reason</u>

"It is a contradiction in terms and ideas to call anything a revelation that comes to us at second hand, either verbally or in writing." Thomas Paine, <u>The Age of Reason</u>

A Practical Guide to Deconstruction

"Of all the systems of religion that ever were invented, there is no more derogatory to the Almighty, more unedifying to man, more repugnant to reason, and more contradictory to itself than this thing called Christianity. Too absurd for belief, too impossible to convince, and too inconsistent for practice, it renders the heart torpid or produces only atheists or fanatics. As an engine of power, it serves the purpose of despotism, and as a means of wealth, the avarice of priests, but so far as respects the good of man, in general, it leads to nothing here or hereafter."— Thomas Paine, <u>The Age of Reason</u>

"The most formidable weapon against errors of every kind is Reason. I have never used any other, and I trust I never shall." Thomas Paine, <u>The Age of Reason</u>

"All national institutions of churches, whether Jewish, Christian, or Turkish, appear to me no other than human inventions set up to terrify and enslave mankind, and monopolize power and profit." Thomas Paine, <u>The Age of Reason</u>

"Whenever we read the obscene stories, the voluptuous

debaucheries, the cruel and torturous executions, the unrelenting vindictiveness, with which more than half the Bible is filled, it would be more consistent that we called it the word of a demon, than the word of God. It is a history of wickedness that has served to corrupt and brutalize mankind; and, for my part, I sincerely detest it, as I detest everything that is cruel."— Thomas Paine, <u>The Age of Reason</u>

"The study of theology, as it stands in Christian churches, is the study of nothing; it is founded on nothing; it rests on no principles; it proceeds by no authorities; it has no data; it can demonstrate nothing; and it admits of no conclusion. Not anything can be studied as a science, without our being in possession of the principles upon which it is founded; and as this is the case with Christian theology, it is therefore the study of nothing." — Thomas Paine, <u>The Age of Reason</u>

"It is a contradiction in terms and ideas, to call anything a revelation that comes to us second-hand, either verbally or in writing. Revelation is necessarily limited to the first communication; after this, it is only an account of something which that person says was a revelation made to him; and though he may find himself obliged to believe it, it cannot be incumbent on me to believe it in the same manner; for it was not a revelation made to *me*, and I have only his word for it that it was made to him."— Thomas Paine, <u>Age of Reason</u>

"Thomas did not believe in the resurrection; and, as they say, would not believe without having ocular and manual demonstration himself. So, neither will I; and the reason is equally as good for me and for every other person as for Thomas." Thomas Paine, <u>Age of Reason</u>

"The age of ignorance commenced with the Christian system." Thomas Paine, <u>Age of Reason</u>

"That many good men have believed this strange fable [Christianity] and lived very good lives under that belief (for credulity is not a crime) is what I have no doubt of. In the first place, they were educated to believe it, and they would have believed anything else in the same manner.

There are also many who have been so enthusiastically enraptured by what they conceived to be the infinite love of God to man, in making a sacrifice of himself, that the vehemence of the idea has forbidden and deterred them from examining into the absurdity and profaneness of the story."— Thomas Paine, <u>The Age of Reason</u>

The Pearl of Great Price

Although we do not hear much about "pearl peeling" today, it was a common practice long ago. This was the process of removing blemishes, stains, and other imperfections from a natural pearl spoiled by imperfections. It required a sharp knife or razor to remove the blemishes and stains. After the "pearl peeling" was completed, only the perfect white pearl remained.

This is like the parable of the pearl of great price. "Again, the kingdom of heaven is like a merchant seeking beautiful pearls, who when he had found one pearl of great price, went and sold all that he had and bought it." Matt 13:45-46 The merchant sold all that he had so he could buy the "one pearl of great price." The merchant had to sell his hokus pokus, false beliefs, and delusional thinking before he could purchase the pearl of great price.

Using Occam's Razors requires critical thinking, asking questions, and cutting out the delusional thinking and hokus pokus. Someone choosing the path of deconstruction can no longer accept "blind faith" as an authoritative answer to meaningful questions. Let knowledge, critical thinking, common sense, and your inner intuition be your friends on your journey.

Fundamentalism

F.E.A.R., or the *false evidence appearing real*, is the outward manifestation of fundamentalism. The Oxford Dictionary describes fundamentalism as "a form of a religion, especially Islam or Protestant Christianity, which upholds belief in the strict, literal interpretation of scripture." At its core, fundamentalism is closed-minded and rigid thinking. Dogmas, doctrines, literalism, and the belief in the inerrancy of scripture are crucial to this narrow-minded thinking.

A fundamentalist is incapable of critical thinking, reasoning, or asking questions. Despite overwhelming evidence that opposes his delusional beliefs, the fundamentalist will not change his dogmatic thinking and continues to believe his views are right. Because most fundamentalists hold on to the literal interpretation of scripture, it suggests this type of thinking is a mental disorder.

Because a "delusion" resembles a mental disorder, we must consider what the mental health community says about it. Psychiatrists and psychologists use a double standard for individuals who manifest the symptoms of a delusion and meet the classical definition of this disorder. They treat individuals with unshakable beliefs that are irrational and unbelievable as a delusional psychotic mental disorder; and ignore billions of people on the planet who believe in a delusional reality of talking snakes, a man living in a whale for 3 days, or a burning bush that talked. The mental health community does not consider a person delusional if their false reality and fantasies are part of a common set of beliefs shared by a larger group.

Author and philosopher Robert M Pirsig said, "When one person suffers from a delusion, it is called insanity. When many people suffer from a delusion, it is called religion." Sigmund Freud suggested that religion was a collective neurosis of mankind.

Herd Mentality

This "collective neurosis" is called herd mentality. It is also called mob mentality or group thinking. The definition of herd mentality is "the tendency of the people in a group to think and behave in ways that conform with others in the group rather than as individuals." (Meriam Webster's Dictionary) One can see this in political views, social behavior, and religion. Belonging to a group of like-minded people provides comfort and social acceptance. The likelihood of judgment, criticism, and social distancing keep individuals locked into the herd. Belonging to the "in crowd" does not mean the herd is always right. History is filled with disturbing examples of a herd mentality gone wild. Racial discrimination, female inequality, bigotry, antisemitism, are just a few examples.

Herd thinking or sheeple behavior is dangerous when it takes away an individual's ability to use critical thinking and form opinions. The definition of sheeple is "people who copy what other people do or believe what they are told and do not think for themselves. Sheeple is a combination of the words sheep and people" Man-made religion has thrived over the centuries because it is based on herd mentality and sheeple behavior. One must accept a set of established dogmas and creeds to belong to the herd. Individuals cannot belong to the herd without accepting the dogmas and creeds sanctioned by the leaders of the flock.

Whether one belongs to a Catholic or Protestant herd, the herd mentality is the same thing, only the outward appearance is different. Both denominations rely on group thinking or a mob mentality to serve the powers controlling the herd. One can argue…

A religion that demands herd thinking is

self-serving and man-made.

Christian deconstruction and deconverting are rapidly growing because individuals reject the authoritarian mindset of institutional religion, which holds them hostage to herd thinking. Many in the "herd" are waking up and sensing something is wrong.

Many factors influence herd mentality. Individuals in

bondage to herd mentality are not consciously aware of their predicament. This is a collective unconsciousness. Later in this book, we will discuss Plato's Allegory of the Cave. The prisoners in the cave are like the "sheeple" or part of the herd mentality. Although one prisoner escaped, the remaining prisoners stayed in the cave because they thought the shadows were real and did not want to leave the "herd."

Crowd psychology is important to herd mentality because people instinctively follow the crowd. More importantly, crowd behavior influences how a person receives information. If the crowd takes on a herd mentality, there is no critical thinking, no questioning, and blissful agreement with the "statement of faith" that defines the beliefs of the herd. A preacher can easily manipulate the crowd by asking the congregation for an affirmative "amen" to his talking points.

Worship music has become a major part of crowd psychology and herd mentality. The music is emotional, scripted, and orchestrated to create a euphoric atmosphere of like-minded people. The music can make people cry, raise their hands, or even jump and down. Repetitive music is manipulative, hypnotic, and used to open one's mind to suggestions. This crowd psychology keeps the congregation in a "herd mentality."

Herd mentality or group thinking is dangerous because it

does not allow individuals to voice their opinions or express opposing viewpoints. Religion is a perfect example of herd mentality and group thinking. Delusional thinking thrives in herd mentality because no one is allowed to ask questions or express a negative opinion.

Spiritual Gaslighting

The definition of gaslighting is "manipulate (someone) using psychological methods into questioning their own sanity or powers of reasoning. This is a modern term that can be applied to Christians who are undergoing deconstruction or deconversion. Spiritual gaslighters are often abusive, manipulative, and closed-minded. It boils down to "We are right, and you are wrong."

In a spiritual context, gaslighting is a form of spiritual abuse where the "know it all" rejects the belief of the person who is deconverting. In most cases, the "know it all" is professing hokus pokus, and the truth seeker is waking up to the truth. A person using spiritual gaslighting will often threaten another by saying something like this…. "You are going to hell if you don't believe like I do," or "You are listening to the devil." The predictable "big bazooka" always comes out as a last resort, "be careful there are false prophets and teachers, and they will deceive many."

Christian gaslighters are working overtime and using every diabolical trick to combat the exodus of free thinkers and deconverters who are leaving the church. Spiritual gaslighting is a common spiritual practice in man-made religions. Truth seekers who are alert, will recognize the gaslighters and the tactics they use to control people and keep power over them. They manipulate a person's sense of spiritual truth and reality by hiding behind blind faith, delusional thinking, and hokus pokus. They also use their ecclesiastical power to shame one into submission and accept their orthodox beliefs.

Spiritual gaslighters tell you what to think without respecting the other person's intelligence, perspective, or experience. Truth-seekers walking the path of deconversion must be aware of "spiritual gaslighters" and the tactics they use to keep individuals in bondage to their way of thinking. Everyone walking the path of deconstruction (the yellow brick road) needs to stay strong and continue to seek truth outside of man-made religion. The inner voice of the mystical Christ inside you makes this reassuring promise for your faith journey. "Howbeit when he, the Spirit of truth, is come, he will guide you into all truth" John 16:13

Because the "voice" of man-made religion is so loud, most unawakened souls have never heard the silent inner voice of the mystical Christ. When you turn off the delusional thinking and hokus pokus of your church, you will soon hear the inner voice of the mystical Christ.

And he said, "Go forth, and stand upon the mount before the Lord. And, behold, the Lord passed by, and a great and strong wind rent the mountains, and brake in pieces the rocks before the Lord; but the Lord was not in the wind: and after the wind an earthquake; but the Lord was not in the earthquake:

And after the earthquake a fire; but the Lord was not in the fire: and after the fire a still small voice.

And it was so, when Elijah heard it, that he wrapped his face in his mantle, and went out, and stood in the entering in of the cave. And, behold, there came a voice unto him, and said, What doest thou here, Elijah? 1 Kings 19 11-13

Elijah stood in the "entering of the cave," just like the prisoner who escaped from Plato's cave and discovered the illuminating light and the True God.

Spiritual Bondage

If your religion teaches you not to question, then it is hiding something from you.

Plato's Allegory of the Cave uses allegory to teach us about individuals who choose to remain in the cave. They believed the shadows on the cave's wall were real and did not want to escape. This is typical of most individuals in man-made religion. They are comfortable and do not want to think for themselves. Because the delusion of the false evidence appearing real has spiritually blinded unawakened souls, the deceptive shadows look real. Plato's allegory reveals a surprising twist to the story.

The other prisoners chained to the wall did not want to escape; they chose to remain in bondage. Metaphorically speaking, the prisoners who did not want to escape represent individuals who refuse "deconstruction." The prisoners are not physically incarcerated, they have the freedom to go anywhere they choose. It is their minds and souls that are in prison. Man-made religion has brainwashed, indoctrinated, and psychologically manipulated the prisoners so they do not want to leave the comfort of their mental prison.

The deconstruction movement is like a "prison ministry" helping unawakened souls exit the cave and come out of spiritual bondage to man-made religion.

The Church has made it extremely difficult to overcome this bondage. Throughout early Church history, one can see the extreme measures taken to control people, spiritually enslave them, and bind them to the whims of papal authority. Anyone who challenged the church's doctrine was labeled a heretic and most often put to death. The religious slave masters burned sacred books and wisdom libraries. They also silenced the ancient Mystery Schools and sanitized the world from all ancient teachings that contradicted the theology of the Roman Church. History records the ugly narrative of the Inquisition, Crusades, and other holy wars to "convert" the population and "bind" them as spiritual slaves to the authoritarian control of the Roman church. Heretics were tortured and burned at the stake to eliminate everyone who disagreed with Rome's theology.

Man-made religion uses more subtle tactics like the fear of hell, literalism, and promises of prosperity and blessings to keep the flock enslaved and shackled to the mental prison walls of the religious "matrix." Churches use entertainment and emotional praise music to "hypnotize" and psychologically sedate the congregation into spiritual ignorance and bondage. Repetitive music allows the counterfeit spirit to take control of the minds of the "prisoners in the cave," so they do not want to leave. The counterfeit spirit is important and will be discussed later in the book.

Even today, man-made religion maintains an ecclesiastical dictatorship as it hides behind its "God given" authority. For example, Catholics give the Vatican ultimate authority to interpret scripture and truth, and Protestant leaders declare their fundamental orthodox ideologies as the inspired "word of God." This is bondage to the religious hierarchy of man-made religion; it requires obedience and religious servitude to remain a church member. The authoritarian rule of man-made religion is a perfect example that illustrates the Latin word "relegare," which means to bind.

In the first Matrix movie, Morpheus told Neo he was born into bondage. The overwhelming power of the "matrix" to program a young person at such an early age makes it extremely difficult to break the chains of bondage.

Morpheus

"As children, we do not separate the possible from the impossible which is why the younger a mind is the easier it is to free while a mind like yours can be very difficult."

Hokus Pokus
A Practical Guide to Deconstruction

St. Ignatius of the Catholic Jesuits said, "Give me a child until he is seven, and I will show you the man." It is far easier for a child to let go of Santa Claus than for an adult Christian to let go of talking snakes, Noah's Ark, Jonah and the whale, and other myths and fables. The indoctrination of literalism into the gullible minds of children creates a mental prison that carries over into adulthood.

Man-made religion indoctrinates children. The definition of indoctrination is the process of teaching a person or group to accept a set of beliefs uncritically. Man-made religion preys on the gullibility of children to believe whatever adults tell them. The leaders of man-made religion know that it is critical to fill the minds of children with hokus pokus because it creates a mental stronghold of delusional thinking that shackles children into spiritual bondage as adults.

Indoctrination of children will make a lot more sense as you continue to read this book. The reader will learn about the counterfeit spirit and the forces behind this brainwashing.

The Pied Piper

When, lo, as they reached the mountainside,

A wondrous portal opened wide,

As if a cavern was suddenly hollowed.

And the Piper advanced, and the children followed,

And when all were into the very last,

The door in the mountainside shut fast.

Robert Browning

The picture of the Pied Piper is a powerful visual aid to illustrate how children and adults are easily led by the counterfeit spirit into a dark spiritual place. Jesus warns us about following blind leaders. He talked about blind religious leaders who lead unawakened souls away from the Kingdom of Heaven. The people following the Pied Piper are blissfully ignorant and have no idea where they will end up.

"Let them alone. They are blind leaders of the blind. And if the blind leads the blind, both will fall into a ditch."

Matt 15:14

Modern Day Pharaohs

The biblical story of the Exodus has striking similarities to the modern-day deconstruction movement. There is a mass "exodus" of individuals walking out the doors of mainstream churches or deconstructing their faith. These individuals are like the Israelite slaves leaving the bondage of Egypt, only this time, it is the bondage of mainstream religion.

Although most historians and scholars agree that the historical Exodus never happened, it always occurs within the consciousness or spirit of a truth seeker. There are both the inner voices of a mystical Moses inside a person calling one out of the bondage of man-made religion; and a mystical pharaoh standing in the way as a gatekeeper, keeping the unawakened soul in bondage to "Egypt" or man-made religion. The mystical Moses says, "Let my children go." The mystical pharaoh inside a person says, "No way," blocking the exit to spiritual freedom like a prison guard demanding that his slaves stay in bondage.

The modern-day "pharaoh" is a tyrant who uses spiritual gaslighting to shackle unawakened souls to man-made religion. It is usually an authority figure, like a pastor, a parent, or a religious zealot within the family, who insists they know better. These modern-day pharaohs are trying to manipulate individuals and control the outcome of their thinking. They will use their Bibles and memorized scripture rebuttals to bully and confuse you. Later in this book, the reader will learn the true identity of the "pharaoh" inside you who is trying to block your exit from the "cave."

Unfortunately, a brand-new deconstructionist is vulnerable to the attacks of the "know it all" and may prematurely give in to the spiritual gaslighters. A truth seeker who spends a minimal amount of time in critical thinking, study, and personal reflection will soon have the confidence, knowledge, and wisdom to stand up and not get pushed around by those spiritual gaslighters who are trying to control you.

Modern Day False Prophets

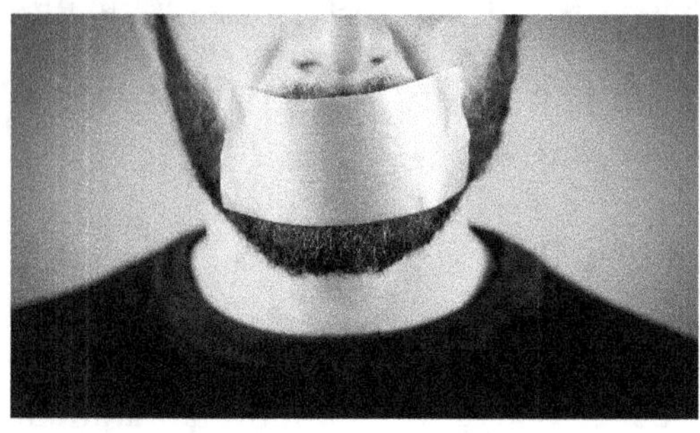 Traditional religion and spiritual gaslighters have silenced the prophets of the modern world. Although Christianity identifies itself with the prophets of the Old Testament, it refuses to acknowledge any outsider who challenges its dogmas, doctrines, and delusional thinking.

Because the members of the Church are so dull of hearing and poisoned by the "apple" of delusion, they cannot comprehend the truth coming out of today's modern-day prophets urging people to wake up and come out of the cave. The message of the modern-day prophets echoes the same criticisms of the "heretics" who opposed the Roman Catholic Church hundreds of years ago. These "holy people" were tortured and burned at the stake to silence them. This will be discussed in greater detail later in the book.

In the past, prophets were labeled heretics. The Roman church (bad fruit) tortured and killed millions of innocent souls in cold blood to protect the "faith." Today spiritual gaslighters who stand behind their pulpits frighten their congregations by suggesting today's prophets are deceivers, scoffers, and false prophets.

Protecting the "faith" is much easier and more humane because the church only needs to metaphorically snap its crooked finger, and the followers do whatever they are told without blinking an eye. Blind faith is the sedative that keeps individuals in spiritual blindness, ignorance, and captivity.

Who Are the Real Scoffers and Deceivers?

Many wolves in sheep's clothing arrogantly point their crooked fingers at modern-day prophets and condemn them for being scoffers and deceivers. One only needs to spend a few minutes in the book of Jeremiah to see and understand that the **pastors** are scattering the sheep and destroying the vineyard. This is another hokus pokus, a sinister cover-up perpetuated by man-made religion to cover up the truth. According to the Bible, **"pastors"** are the real scoffers and deceivers because they are the ones who scatter the sheep, destroy the vineyard, and transgress against the True God.

The counterfeit spirit prevents unawakened souls from discerning the truth and recognizing what Jeremiah is saying to those with ears to hear. Pastors are preventing people from knowing the True God and driving unawakened souls away.

Jeremiah 23:1-2 Woe be unto the **_pastors_** that destroy and scatter the sheep of my pasture, saith the LORD. Therefore, thus saith the LORD God of Israel against the **_pastors_** that feed my people; Ye have scattered my flock and driven them away.

Jer_2:8 The priests said not, where is the LORD? And they that handle the law knew me not: the **_pastors_** also transgressed against me, and the prophets prophesied by Baal, and walked after things that do not profit.

Hokus Pokus
A Practical Guide to Deconstruction

Jer_12:10 Many ***pastors*** have destroyed my vineyard, they have trodden my portion underfoot, they have made my pleasant portion a desolate wilderness.

Jer_23:1 Woe be unto the ***pastors*** that destroy and scatter the sheep of my pasture saith the LORD.

Jer_23:2 Therefore thus saith the LORD God of Israel against the ***pastors*** that feed my people; Ye have scattered my flock, and driven them away, and have not visited them: behold, I will visit upon you the evil of your doings, saith the LORD.

Individuals going through a "faith deconversion" need to turn this false accusation around and understand that man-made religion is the "false prophet," keeping people from knowing the truth revealed by Jesus of Nazareth and embraced by many of the earliest Christians.

In the Matrix movie, Morpheus warned Neo that by taking the red pill, he would show him how deep down the rabbit hole goes… and that all he was offering was the truth. Metaphorically taking the "red pill" opens your eyes, and you begin to see things from a new perspective. One is empowered to disregard group thinking and question everything. The "red pill" is a symbol for waking up to the truth. This phenomenon is growing exponentially in Christian churches as more people wake up and experience enlightenment and spiritual freedom. Individuals are discovering the "key of knowledge" or gnosis that the Roman Church took away two thousand years ago.

Truth Detector

If you still find yourself lost in the deconstruction maze. You can always follow the words of Jesus of Nazareth and let them guide you.

"Beware of false prophets, who come to you in sheep's clothing, but inwardly they are ravenous wolves. You will know them by their fruits. Do men gather grapes from thornbushes or figs from thistles? Even so, every good tree bears good fruit, but a bad tree bears bad fruit. A good tree cannot bear bad fruit, nor can a bad tree bear good fruit. Every tree that does not bear good fruit is cut down and thrown into the fire. Therefore, by their fruits you will know them." Matt 7 15-20 The "bad fruits" and "bad trees" will be discussed at great length later in the book .It will be easy to spot the false prophets who come in sheep's clothing but are inwardly ravenous wolves.

The bad fruits are the bloodshed, corruption, materialism, scandals, and other hokus pokus that are out in the open and impossible to deny. Throughout history thousands of innocent souls were labeled heretics and tortured or burned at the stake by the Roman Church. Jesus of Nazareth is clearly pointing his finger at the bad fruit of man-made religion and warning unawakened souls to stay away from them.

Fundamentalism

Most often the counterfeit spirit keeps individuals locked into the comfort of belonging to the herd. In Plato's Allegory of the Cave, only one prisoner chose to leave the cave and the other prisoners remained in the bondage of the cave staring at shadows. Although the message of the "bad fruits" and "bad trees" is easy to understand, it has failed to make a significant impact on modern day church attendees. The counterfeit spirit seduces individuals to remain in man-made religion stained with bloodshed, corruption, materialism, scandals, and other hokus pokus. The counterfeit spirit will be discussed in greater detail later in the book.

Fearmongering

The definition of fearmongering is "the action of intentionally trying to make people afraid of something when this is not necessary or reasonable. (Cambridge dictionary) A popular perception of many outspoken people discussing religion is that it is based on fear. A famous writer and philosopher, Bertrand Russel, wrote, "Religion is based, I think, primarily and mainly upon fear." The fear of hell, the fear of not being good enough, or the fear of being "left behind" at the rapture are just a few examples of the "fear" that torments the minds of many believers. "In addition to the widely accepted meaning of "fear" as a strong unpleasant emotion in response to a danger or threat, there is an equally important acronym, F.E.A.R is false evidence appearing real. This will be discussed in greater detail later in the book.

Dante's Divine Comedy stands out as one of the great classics of literature. It was written in the 14th century to portray the eternal damnation of hell. Although this was written over seven hundred years ago, it had a profound and lasting influence that still terrorizes people in the modern world. In his poem, he described the nine circles of hell and the fitting punishment assigned to the sinners. His poem about the horrors of eternal damnation is an example of fearmongering and scaremongering used by the Catholic and Protestant Churches to control the world's population.

Fearmongering or scaremongering has been a tool for Christians to recruit new members and keep current members in bondage to the dogmas and creeds of the faith. Billy Graham was a Southern Baptist evangelist who has been portrayed as one of the most influential Christian leaders of the twentieth century. He hosted meetings between 1947 and 2005. The Billy Graham Association claims that Billy Graham preached the gospel message to more people than anyone else. Nearly 215 million people in more than 185 countries attended his meetings. He hosted 417 crusades. One can also argue that he was the greatest fearmonger and scaremonger of all time.

His fire and brimstone preaching scared the "hell" out of people. He preached that hell is real and that God would judge everyone when they died. Sinners would go to their eternal damnation if they did not accept Jesus of Nazareth as lord and Savior. In one of his sermons, he said, "God is a God of wrath, and His wrath is going to be poured out upon this world and upon you if you are outside of Christ." His fearmongering crusades would climax in scripted and orchestrated altar calls. Billy Graham's captivating sermon scared people. Because the promise of going to heaven when a person dies was a "no-brainer," the crowds emptied their seats when the invitation to come forward was announced. The song, Just as I Am, was always played during the altar call. Because music has been described as an effective type of hypnosis, the melody and words of the song created a hypnotic atmosphere that spoke to the crowd and urged people to come forward. Billy Graham was a master at using psychological manipulation to justify the outward appearance of saving people for Christ.

Although millions of people thought they were saved and would go to heaven, Billy Graham admitted that few people became committed Christians. "And yet, in a 1990 interview with PBS, Billy Graham stated his belief that only about 25% of those who came forward at one of his events became Christians. ("Reverend Billy Graham talking with David Frost," PBS, January 23, 1993, as recorded in David Frost's Billy Graham - Personal Thoughts of a Public Man, (1997), pp.71-72) Although Billy Graham touched a significant number of lives, his "fearmongering" cannot be overlooked. Does the end justify the means? Ask yourself does God condone "fearmongering"? Did Jesus of Nazareth instruct his disciples to "scare the hell of them" when he sent them out to preach the kingdom of heaven? Fearmongering is a psychological tool of man-made religion.

"In recent years, studies have shown that only 3-6% of people who "come forward" at an evangelistic crusade are any different in their beliefs or behavior one year later." (Pulpit & Pen, Do Greg Laurie's Harvest Crusades Produce False Converts? June 22, 2016) This suggest that a spontaneous decision for Christ is most often a false conversion.

Everyone watching, in person or on TV, was amazed at all the lines of people going forward to recite the sinner's prayer and invite Jesus into their hearts. Although they thought they were committing their lives to Jesus, we now know that only a tiny fraction of the people made a lasting commitment. Billy Graham's altar calls were fabrications that fooled everyone. Although a tiny fraction of people benefited from the altar call, the vast majority were unchanged. It was false evidence appearing real that deceived everyone watching.

False Evidence Appearing Real

The letters in the acronym F.E.A.R. create a useful tool to help one remember the definition of a delusion. It stands for False Evidence Appearing Real. Both serve and mutually support one another. F.E.A.R (false evidence appearing real) perpetuates fear (unpleasant emotion.)

Because Santa Clause is a universal figure, he perfectly fits the narrative about F.E.A.R. or false evidence appearing real. Through the eyes of a child, Santa Clause is a real person who has a long snowy white beard and dresses in a red jacket trimmed with white fur. He lives at the North Pole and flies through the sky in a sled pulled by nine reindeer. Parents bring their children to see Santa in person so they can personally tell him what they want for Christmas. Because children are guided by childish thinking, they believe what their parents and other adults tell them… Santa is real.

In most cases, parents are the first adults to introduce Santa to their children. Parents, grandparents, teachers, and other adults perpetuate this fantasy by telling "little white lies" that trick the child into believing fictitious stories about Santa Claus.

Eventually, every parent must tell the truth, "Santa Claus is not real." We can learn a lot from our children. Despite their age and immaturity, they ask questions and want to know the truth. Can we say the same for most adults?

F.E.A.R.

One must first understand that the ancient world had a deep intuitive understanding of spiritual truths. They understood that the stories about their pagan deities were mythological, allegorical, and symbolic. Nature, the zodiac, philosophy, and mathematics were sources of their wisdom. Sacred mystery schools throughout the ancient world taught initiates about man's relationship with the True God. This wisdom has a long history going back thousands of years to ancient Egypt. Some of the greatest spiritual minds shared this knowledge and passed it on through secret writings, rituals, and drama plays. The most common themes centered around the symbolic birth, death, and resurrection of a deity. Drama plays or writings like the gospels were symbolic scripts used in initiation ceremonies for advanced initiates. They were not intended to be comprehended as literal stories and events but as allegories and esoteric teachings.

Because it is crucial that the reader understands this important point it will be repeated. Initiates were instructed that these allegories were not literal stories, but spiritual teachings hidden in esoteric symbolisms. Because this knowledge was sacred, it took several initiations to communicate the esoteric knowledge to the initiates who were seeking a deeper relationship with the True

God. The mysteries were not revealed to the masses because this knowledge or gnosis was never shared with the population on the outside. The initiates took a solemn oath to keep their knowledge about the mysteries a secret, and they would never share these teachings with anyone outside the mystery school.

The false evidence appearing real was the counterfeit spirit that tricked the world into believing the delusional thinking and hokus pokus of the early church. The Roman Catholic Church was financially supported and politically empowered by the mighty power of the Roman Empire. The merging of the secular state and the church allowed the false evidence appearing real to go unchallenged. This diabolical marriage created a man-made religion (know them by their fruits) that was free to create all sorts of hokus pokus and delusional thinking.

Because the new converts were uneducated peasants, they were easy prey for Roman Catholic missionaries. The nobility received large sums of money and other benefits as bribery from the church state to buy their conversion and allegiance. This allowed the Catholic Church to dominate the world for hundreds of years despite the corruption, materialism, and scandals of the priests, bishops, and papacy.

The false evidence appearing real was a useful decoy for the early church to recruit new members. Because large numbers of unawakened souls multiplied throughout the world, a "collective unconsciousness" became the new normal for "believers." This is like the "prisoners" in Plato's cave since childhood who believed the shadows on the wall were real.

The false evidence appearing real will be discussed in greater detail later in the book. This is only the tip of the iceberg.

Religion and Spirituality

There are thousands of religions throughout the world. Each one is unique and adheres to a particular belief system. Nearly all of them are rooted in ethnicity and geographical location. This means one's origin of birth will determine an individual's religious affiliation. For example, someone born in Greece will grow up in the Greek Orthodox faith, someone born in Iraq will be a Muslim, and a baby born in Mexico will be a Catholic. The four major religions are Christianity, Islam, Hinduism, and Buddhism. These religions are the largest and account for over 77% of the world's population. Although not recognized as a "religion," the secular, nonreligious, agnostic, and atheist group is the third largest. Archeological remains suggest that some form of religion existed thousands of years ago when a primitive man walked the earth.

The importance of religion cannot be dismissed because it serves humanity in many beneficial ways. It has influenced our morals, behavior, and social evolution. It has also filled man's innate desire to reach out to a divine being. One thing that stands out as a common denominator among religions is a strong belief that their ideology is right, and all the others are wrong.

The idea that both Plato's Allegory of the Cave and Morpheus in the Matrix movie are making about being a slave is also portrayed in the Bible. Because Gnostic Paul does not want the

reader to take his writing literally, he makes it very clear and says….
"This is an allegory." (The Church has ignored this important word and continues to cover it up.) Gnostic Paul wrote, "Now this is an _allegory_: these women are two covenants. One woman is Hagar, from Mount Sinai, bearing children for slavery. Now Hagar is Mount Sinai in Arabia and corresponds to the present Jerusalem, for she is in <u>slavery</u> with her children. But the other woman corresponds to the Jerusalem above; she is <u>free</u>, and she is our mother." Gal 4:24-26 To summarize what Gnostic Paul says, one covenant represents slavery and bondage, and the other is free and alive. In modern times, religion is "bondage and in slavery with her children," and spirituality is "free and corresponds to the Jerusalem above."

The Latin word for religion is "relegare," which means to bind. In contrast, the Latin word for spirituality is "spiritus, "meaning breath, soul, vigor, or to be alive. The words, "religion" and "spirituality," are not the same nor interchangeable: one is in bondage and the other is free and alive.

Jesus of Nazareth is considered a great teacher by his followers. In the four gospels, he was called "teacher" 60 times. It is ironic that he is called a great teacher, and the crowds still did not understand what he was teaching.

One third of his teachings were spoken in parables. Jesus'

disciples came and said to him, "Why do you use parables when you speak to the crowds?" Jesus replied, "Because they haven't received the secrets of the kingdom of heaven, but you have. For those who have will receive more and they will have more than enough. But as for those who don't have, even the little they have will be taken away from them. This is why I speak to the crowds in parables: although they see, they don't really see; and although they hear, they don't really hear or understand." Matt 13: 10-13

According to Jesus of Nazareth, one must receive the secrets of the kingdom of heaven to understand the parables. He pointed to his disciples and said, "to you it has been granted to know the mysteries to the kingdom of heaven, and then he pointed to *those people* and said it has not been granted. Individuals reading their Bibles literally are "*those people*" who do not understand the kingdom of heaven, "although they see, they really don't see; and although they hear, they really don't understand."

Is it possible that the Gospel writers disguised their text in literalism or a literal story for "*those people*" who have not received the secrets of the kingdom of heaven? But to those who received the secrets of the kingdom of heaven it was a parable teaching ancient esoteric knowledge and gnosis.

Man-made religion is based on a standardized system of dogmas, doctrines, and structured beliefs that enslave individuals into bondage. It is most often associated with individuals who share a common faith. Religious institutions and their hierarchy determine morals, ethics, and predefined core beliefs. Members of the Church organization must follow specific rules and regulations to be accepted into the group. Traditional religion relies on blind faith and discourages critical thinking, common sense, and asking questions. It also promises a heavenly reward or eternal punishment when one dies to keep unawakened souls trapped in spiritual ignorance and bondage to the delusional thinking and hokus pokus of man-made religion.

Spirituality is about the inner self and discovering one's personal beliefs outside of traditional religion. Personal study, critical thinking, and listening to one's inner voice empower individuals to discover the truth, even if it does not follow traditional and mainstream thinking. "Spirituality" rejects man-made theologies, doctrines, dogmas, and predefined beliefs. It teaches people to constantly listen to their inner voice. Spirituality is a solitary experience of the divine and does not require a group of people to reinforce one's beliefs. It is a personal experience that may change and evolve over one's lifetime. Nothing is set in stone. Spirituality looks within and becomes one with God and all creation; it is an internal journey and not an external ritual.

Worship is not directed to some person in the heavens but to one's higher self or the mystical Christ within. "But woe to you, scribes and Pharisees, hypocrites! For you shut the kingdom of heaven in people's faces. _For you neither enter yourselves nor allow those who would enter to go in_." Matt 25:13 Spirituality is universal and unites all people regardless of their beliefs and traditions. It is based on freedom and one's direct experience of the soul to know when something is true, as opposed to accepting the predefined beliefs of someone with ecclesiastical authority. Spirituality transcends fear, guilt, condemnation, and delusional thinking, exchanging them for higher consciousness, the Mind of Christ, or the Mystical "Christ Within."

This comparison between "religion" and "spirituality" shows the drastic differences, but more importantly, it suggests why there is an exodus of Christians leaving the Church. According to the Pew Research Center study, the number of Christians in America has dropped from 90% to 64% in the last 50 years. Pew Research also reported that 27% of U.S. adults now say they are "spiritual but not religious." This is confirmation that there is a "spiritual awakening" in America as both younger and older individuals are rapidly pulling away from man-made religion. More people are rejecting the "religion" they inherited from their parents, deconstructing their faith, and tearing down the curtain of "blind faith."

Deconstruction is a Good Thing

Faith "deconstruction" is a modern Christian phenomenon where people rethink and examine their core beliefs. Because more individuals are experiencing a divine calling to "fact check" their Christian beliefs, deconstruction has become widespread and growing. The church hierarchy is threatened by anyone who asks meaningful questions and tries to explain this undeniable exodus with hokus pokus arguments.

A predictable response warns members to be fearful of the deconstruction movement and stay away from it. The ultimate destination of deconstruction is a search for a meaningful, truthful, and spiritually mature faith. Therefore, one's journey is a good thing. One may find that you have spiritually outgrown your current faith and need to move on to something else, or you may find that your current faith passes the test, and it is right for you. This means either way, one wins.

Deconstruction of the faith does not mean you go to your pastor for answers because he is a biased defender of the Christian faith. Although he may silently agree with the ideas of a truth seeker, he is obligated to remain loyal and defend the hokus pokus. Deconstruction requires looking outside one's comfort zone to read and study non-Christian material and resources. There are countless videos online that provide valuable information. Deconstructing your faith may take a few days, months, or even years because every individual is different. Most people feel good about cleaning out the garage or their closet, faith deconstruction is cleaning out one's spiritual closet of hokus pokus and delusional thinking.

Plato's Allegory of the Cave uses allegory to teach us that deconstruction is absolutely necessary for the soul's ascent to illumination or enlightenment. The prisoner who escaped bondage had to make a steep and difficult climb out of the cave. His journey upward is a metaphor for his faith deconstruction. He had to recognize his delusional thinking was false, and the shadows in the cave were not real. It took courage and fortitude for the prisoner to escape the shackles of bondage and climb out of the cave. His "deconstruction" allowed him to reach the opening of the cave and for the first time, see the brilliant illuminating light or the True God.

Waking Up in Aquarius

The 5th Dimension recorded one of the most popular songs of 1969. The lyrics talked about the dawning of a new Age and referred to the "mind's true liberation."

Harmony and understanding

Sympathy and trust abounding

No more falsehoods or derisions

Golden living dreams of visions

Mystic crystal revelation

And the mind's true liberation

Aquarius

Aquarius

Age of Aquarius
5th Dimension 1969

Follow The Man with The Water Pitcher

"And he said unto them, behold when ye are entered into the city, there shall meet you a man bearing a pitcher of water; follow him into the house whereinto he goeth. Luke 22:10The Zodiac sign of Aquarius is the "man with a water pitcher." The Gospel writers were brilliant thinkers familiar with the cosmos, mythology, and mystical truths.

Ancient civilizations pointed to the Age of Aquarius for "true liberation" and spiritual enlightenment. Many individuals will be called out of bondage by this energy and "baptized" in the sacred waters pouring out of Aquarius. Hokus pokus and delusional thinking will be washed away and replaced with truth and enlightenment.

The dictionary describes the Age of Aquarius as an astrological era believed to bring increased spirituality and harmony on earth. It is like the universe opens a cosmic window that opens and pours out rays of truth and spiritual enlightenment on our planet.

Hokus Pokus
A Practical Guide to Deconstruction

Some skeptics are prone to dismiss this as nonsense, while others will embrace Aquarius as a powerful source of spiritual enlightenment and growth.

Sometime during the Age of Aquarius, there will be a major change in thinking similar to the Protestant Reformation. Members of man-made religion will need to make a choice between the hokus pokus and delusional thinking of Christianity or follow the man with the water pitcher who offers truth, understanding, and the mind's true liberation.

Ancient Gnostics gazed at the nighttime sky and discovered the fingerprints of the Divine embedded in the Zodiac. They saw the "life of Christ" written in the heavens. The ancients identified twelve major constellations that mirror the life of the "Christos." The sun passing through each constellation symbolized a spiritual marker in the heavens.

This is a very short version of this celestial journey of the sun as it passes through the Zodiac. It is called "astrotheology." The sun passes through Virgo, which is the sign of the virgin. As the sun continues its journey through the Zodiac, it is "baptized" in Aquarius by the man with the water pitcher. The sun eventually goes through the minor constellation of Crux, which has four bright stars in the shape of a cross, commonly referred to as the Southern Cross.

Waking Up in Aquarius

The ancient teachers who lived thousands of years ago said the sun was "crucified" each year between the two thieves of Sagittarius and Capricorn. On December 21^{st,} the sun visually stood still for three days, died, and was resurrected on December 25th. This is commonly called the winter solstice. One can study astrotheology and learn more about the "signs" in the heavens.

Our modern scientists have the Hubbell Telescope to map the skies, but there is no comparison to the esoteric wisdom and knowledge handed down to us by these brilliant people. Unlike our contemporary astronomers and scientists, the ancient astronomers were spiritually enlightened. They understood that the Zodiac was a mirror to the soul. This was referred to in the ancient saying that has been handed down throughout history… "So Above So Below."

The constellations move in a very slow procession that takes about two thousand years to complete. We are just leaving The Age of Pisces, which is associated with the sign of the fish and the Christian era and beginning our transition into the Age of Aquarius. Many believe this will cause a major shift in the consciousness of mankind causing old beliefs to fall away and new ones to take their place. We already see evidence of this as individuals experience unexplained psychic phenomena. The Age of Aquarius is a time of questioning things and exploring new ideas. More people are soul-searching and trying to sort things out; asking themselves if their core beliefs inherited at birth still make sense as an adult.

The Dead Sea Scrolls

The Dawning of the Age of Aquarius may have started in 1945, near Nag Hammadi, Egypt. Perhaps it was Aquarius who led a young teenage boy to a collection of clay jars hidden in the caves of Qumran. The discovery of these manuscripts is one of the most significant archeological discoveries in modern times. It is estimated the Nag Hammadi documents were hidden around 390 CE. and escaped the destruction of the Roman Church. It was like discovering a time capsule with priceless information about the spiritual beliefs of first-century believers. In 1947 a second discovery near Qumran and the Dead Sea brought to light another considerable number of scrolls. Although the Catholic Church tried to hide these documents from the public, their efforts were unsuccessful. Many of the manuscripts reveal teachings that drastically differ from the views of man-made religion. They teach about the spark of the Divine or the Christos who lives within every person, and the evil rulers and counterfeit spirit that deceives humanity.

Waking Up in Aquarius

These two manuscript libraries contain the Gnostic Gospels that give a very different perspective on Jesus and his disciples. In many ways, these manuscripts reveal teachings that challenge the literal interpretation of Scripture. These ancient gospels clearly reveal the devious agenda of the Roman Church to destroy the evidence and the credibility of the early Gnostics. Leaders and apologists of the mainstream church continue to keep individuals away from these manuscripts by attacking the credibility of the documents and suggesting that they are heretical. This keeps unawakened souls spiritually ignorant and blind to the true faith of the earliest believers of the first century. The Gnostic gospels demonstrate that the literal understanding of the Old and New Testament by the Roman Church is a misrepresentation of the true "teachings" taught by Jesus.

It is no random coincidence that this monumental discovery occurred at just the precise time in human history when the Age of Aquarius and the man with the water pitcher appeared in our nighttime sky. This is the Dawning of the Age of Aquarius and the beginning of mankind's true liberation from the bondage of delusion and spiritual ignorance.

The Catholic Church banned the Gnostic Gospels and many other illuminating books to hide the wisdom, truth, and beliefs of the earliest Christians. These gospels are a great source for learning.

Internet

We can also look to the birth of the internet as evidence that the Dawning of the Age of Aquarius is not only pouring out wisdom and truth but also giving us the technology to "preach" the Gospel of the Kingdom to all nations. The official birthday of the internet is January 1, 1983. Before this, computer networks did not have a standard way to communicate with each other. A new protocol was introduced on this date which was known as TCP/IP. This created a universal language that allowed all networks to "talk" with each other.

The internet blew open the doors to information and knowledge. The Age of Aquarius may be the source of this revolutionary information resource. Aquarius is waking up millions of truth seekers worldwide. Souls waking up in Aquarius can now go online and find meaningful answers to their spiritual questions. Access to the internet exposes "blind faith" as a psychological tool of the mainstream church to keep people in spiritual ignorance.

"And this Gospel of the Kingdom shall be preached in all the world for a witness unto *all nations,* and then shall the end come." Matt 24:14

Spiritually Woke

Another undeniable example demonstrating how the Age of Aquarius impacts our secular world is the "woke culture" and "cancel culture" movements. Sources point to a 1962 New York Times article that used "woke." It was added to the dictionary in 2017. There is an invisible energy that is just like the invisible rays of the sun and moon that impact the waves of our oceans. This cosmic energy changes how people think about racial injustice, inequality, and other important issues. The slang word "Woke" is evidence that society is truly waking up and taking steps to correct the problems of racial discrimination.

It took a tragic event on May 25, 2020, for the world to "woke" up to the brutality of racial injustice. A police officer placed a knee on the neck of an African American for 8 minutes and 46 seconds. Although Mr. Floyd cried out "I cannot breathe, the police officer continued to bear down. The world was horrified by the murder and reacted with civil unrest and riots.

The Age of Aquarius is just dawning; we have already seen the "woke culture" and "cancel culture" emerging worldwide. "Woke" is a slang word that originated in the African American community as a substitution for waking up or awaken. The modern word "woke" is defined as "Aware of and actively attentive to important facts and issues (especially issues of racial and social justice)." Although the word has its roots in racial injustice and social discrimination, the momentum of the "woke culture" is expanding into all sectors of modern society, including education, business, professional sports, and government… and spirituality.

The dawning of the Age of Aquarius has given birth to a growing number of "spiritually woke" individuals. An undeniable shift in consciousness is taking place in our world. Research points to a mass exodus of Christians leaving churches. This emerging group of souls who are waking up has been labeled "none" because they have no religious affiliation. They are leaving the spiritual bondage of the "cave" because Aquarius is showing them the shadows in front of them are not real.

Progressive Christianity

Another example of the Age of Aquarius pouring out truth and enlightenment on the planet is the birth of Progressive Christianity. This resembles the fracturing of the Catholic Church during the Protestant Reformation. We are now witnessing a split between the fundamental right-wing Christians and the emerging progressive Christians.

The Center for Progressive Christianity was founded in 1994 by Jim Adams. His vision was to reach the growing number of people leaving the church because they felt man-made religion was irrelevant and repressive. In a few short years, the organization had a long list of churches and clergy worldwide who share this common bond.

Because many of their beliefs are a radical departure from fundamental Christianity, Progressives are viewed as heretical and liberal by the right-wing establishment. Right wing fundamentalists are viciously attacking this new group and trying to discredit the movement. They hide behind their biblical literalism, absolute certainty, and blissful ignorance to convince their followers that the Progressives are false prophets and a sign of the "end times."

Hokus Pokus
A Practical Guide to Deconstruction

Most hard-core Christians are too arrogant and closed minded, to look into the mirror and see they are the problem. This may turn out to be a good thing for Progressive Christianity because more people will recognize the delusional thinking and hokus pokus of fundamental dogmas and rigid beliefs.

Progressive Christianity does not consider the Bible infallible or inerrant; they believe it was written by inspired human beings. Progressives also reject biblical literalism and look to the allegories, metaphors, and symbolisms for a deeper interpretation of Scripture. Many reject the doctrine of original sin and believe souls are not inherently sinful and separated from God. Some reject the idea that God required a blood sacrifice of his "only Son" to forgive the sins of humanity; therefore, Jesus did not need to die for our atonement of sin or "missing the mark." Many Progressives also believe the literal resurrection story is a spiritual metaphor.

Progressive Christianity questions traditions and embraces the Sacredness and Oneness of life. It is tolerant of other faiths and views the teachings of Jesus as one of many diverse ways to experience wisdom. They welcome all people regardless of sexual orientation, ethnic background, and religious orientation. Peace and justice in the world are important to them. They do not bend their knees to blind faith but value critical thinking, questioning things, and learning.

Progressive Christianity is removing the veil of literalism from fundamental right-wing Christianity and exposing the dogmas, doctrines, fundamental beliefs, and hokus pokus that keep unawakened souls in bondage to their orthodox beliefs.

The waters pouring out of Aquarius will "pull the ecclesiastical robes" off the religious literalists and expose their delusion and lies. The fairy tale, The Emperor Has No Clothes describes an emperor tricked into believing he was wearing invisible magical clothes; all his nobility and the people in the streets encouraged this fantasy. A little child said, "But he doesn't have anything on."

Because literalism has spiritually blinded unawakened souls, the Age of Aquarius will usher in a dramatic shift of consciousness that allows people to see literalism as "childish" thinking. They will discover that man-made religion has given humanity spiritual milk, not solid food. Aquarius will remove the veil of literalism and reveal the Divine Truth hidden in the Bible's metaphors, allegories, and spiritual imagery. It will remove spiritual blindness and wake people up to the "things" Jesus taught.

Wonderful Wizard of Oz

"I don't believe you!"

The Wonderful Wizard of Oz is a children's novel written in 1900 by L. Frank Baum. It was later made into a movie in 1939 starring Judy Garland, Ray Bolger, Bert Lahr, Jack Haley, Frank Morgan, and Toto. It was MGM's most expensive production back then, costing around 2.7 million dollars. The movie included 124 adults and twenty-four children that were credited as Munchkins. It was the very first movie filmed in Technicolor. The song *Over the Rainbow* remains one of the most famous songs ever. When people cannot find the right words because something is beyond expression, quotes from the movie often come to mind, like "That's a horse of a different color" and "we're not in Kansas anymore."

There are many quotes from the Wizard of Oz that deserve special attention. Here are a few:

"Someplace where there isn't any trouble. Do you suppose there is such a place, Toto? There must be." Dorothy

"If I ever go looking for my heart's desire again, I won't look any further than my own backyard. Because if it isn't there, I never lost it to begin with" Is that right?" Dorothy

"You always had the power, my dear; you just had to learn it for yourself." Glenda

"Pay no attention to that man behind the curtain." — The Wizard of Oz

"I don't believe you." Dorothy

"You humbug!" Scarecrow

"That's exactly so I'm a humbug." Wizard of Oz

"There's no place like home." Dorothy

"Toto, we're home. Home! And this is my room, and you're all here. And I'm not gonna leave here ever, ever again, because I love you all, and - oh, Auntie Em - there's no place like home!" Dorothy

"A heart is shown not by how much you love, but by how

much you are loved by others." — The Wizard of Oz

Researchers at the University of Turin in Italy studied 47,000 movies and named Wizard of Oz as the most influential movie of all time. (Yahoo News Nov 30, 2018) The public has a love affair with the Wizard of Oz movie. The magic of Dorothy, Scarecrow, Cowardly Lion, Tin Man, and Toto have captivated viewers for decades. What is the underlying connection that draws both children and adults to this iconic movie?

L. Frank Baum

Because of L. Frank Baum and his wife disapproved of man-made religion; they joined the Theosophy Society in 1892, about eight years before he wrote The Wizard of Oz. The term "theosophy" is derived from the Greek theos, "god, gods, or divine," and Sophia, "wisdom." It is understood the term means "divine wisdom." "It encourages open-minded inquiry into world religions, philosophy, science, and the arts to understand the wisdom of the ages, respect all life, and help people explore spiritual transformation." (Mission Statement Theosophical Society in America) Theosophy is not a religion. (They are like the ancient Gnostics who pursued gnosis and Divine esoteric wisdom.) They believe a lack of knowledge about higher truths makes one see things from the wrong perspective. (This is like Plato's Allegory of the Cave, where the prisoners only saw shadows and believed they were real.) Theosophy values study, meditation, and service to others. According to Theosophy, the term "Christ" means the personal divinity "indwelling" each individual human." (Wikipedia)

It should be apparent that The Wonderful Wizard of Oz is not a children's novel. It is an allegorical tale with layers of symbolism and hidden messages. The Wonderful Wizard of Oz is about the soul's journey to spiritual awakening and enlightenment on the Yellow Brick Road. It is written on two levels. The first level is a children's novel, and the second level is esoteric spiritual wisdom.

The Wizard of Oz is a modern-day example of how the ancient mystery schools, Gnostic Paul, and other spiritual masters disguised their esoteric message. The gospel writers also used this method to disguise the inner voice of the mystical Christ. Many scholars believe that the Gospel of John is Gnostic. "Gnosticism taught that salvation came from gnosis secret knowledge, and Gnostics did not see Jesus as a savior but a revealer of knowledge. The gospel teaches that salvation can only be achieved through revealed wisdom, specifically belief in (literally belief *into*) Jesus. John's picture of a supernatural savior who promised to return to take those who believed in him to a heavenly dwelling could be *fitted into Gnostic view"* (Wikipedia)

It is the inner mystical Christ who is talking to those with ears to hear; others on the outside hear the human voice of the historical Jesus of Nazareth and mistakenly take his words literally. The Mystical Christ is the inner spiritual voice from within that speaks to those with ears to hear.

Who do you hear in this Bible passage? Do you hear the voice of a physical person who lived two thousand years ago or the inner voice of the Mystical Christ within you? "I am the way and the truth and the life. No one comes to the Father except through me."

L. Frank Braun, like Gnostic Paul and others, hid their message from the masses because it was holy, and people would make fun of it.

"Do not give that which is holy to dogs, and do not throw your pearls before pigs, for they will trample them under their feet, and turn and tear you to pieces."

Matt 7:6

Hokus Pokus

A Practical Guide to Deconstruction

This is a brief introduction to the symbolism in The Wizard of Oz. There are numerous books, articles, and videos that explore the spiritual symbolism of the Wizard of Oz.

Here is a partial list of the symbolisms that L. Frank Baum used in his allegory.

- Dorothy Gale represents the soul.

- Toto means whole in Latin. He is the spiritual intuition that guides the soul.

- Glinda is the Good Witch of the North, representing the divine feminine who looks out for Dorothy. She is the love and guiding light who is within every person.

- The ruby slippers were originally silver. This represented the "silver cord" that philosophers and mystics use to express the connection between our physical and spiritual astral bodies.

- The Wicked Witch of the East represents old, shattered beliefs.

- The Wicked Witch of the West represents oppression, tyranny, and fear.

- The Scarecrow represents our intellect, thoughts, and thirst for knowledge.

- The Tin Man represents our emotions, compassion, and empathy.

- The Lion represents courage and the importance of taking bold action.

- The Wizard represents organized religion and is personified as a fraud. He also symbolizes the rulers of this world and powers of darkness who control the thoughts and actions of humanity. This will be discussed later in the book.

- The Yellow Brick Road is the spiritual path that leads one to enlightenment or awakening.

- The song Over the Rainbow refers to a bridge that reaches between earth and the spirit realm.

Hokus Pokus
A Practical Guide to Deconstruction

Poppies are associated with sleep and symbolize ignorance, the unawakened soul, or a lower level of consciousness. Dorothy and the Cowardly Lion mysteriously fell into a deep sleep when they walked through the poppy field. This is a metaphor for the common theme of falling into a deep "spiritual sleep." Blind faith, literalism, and hokus pokus are like the "poppies" who put unawakened souls into a deep "spiritual sleep."

A tornado dropped Dorothy Gale into the Land of Oz. Often a traumatic experience, loss, or turbulent event in life drops one into the "Land of Oz." Difficult times in life often prompt the unawakened soul to walk the "Yellow Brick Road." The most painful times in life are often like childbirth giving birth to a spiritual awakening and enlightenment.

Dorothy's journey on the Yellow Brick Road may also represent the path of deconstruction and deconversion because it requires the soul to fight off the evil witch and flying monkeys that want to keep the soul in bondage.

Like the fairy tale "The Emperor with No Clothes," The Great Wizard (man-made religion) fooled everyone. Toto pulled back the curtain and revealed that the Wizard was a fraud who was a grandiose hoaxster spouting lies and delusional thinking. The Wizard was powerless and incapable of helping Dorothy Gale find her way home. He could not save her. A little child said about the emperor without clothes, "But he hasn't got anything on." Spiritually "waking up" is allowing the little child inside you or "the inner voice of "Toto" to sound the alarm, "But he hasn't got anything on."

Spiritual awakening or enlightenment is pulling back the curtain and discovering the truth, even if it is not something you want to hear. It is like the prisoner who escaped in Plato's cave realizing the "shadows" are not real, and Dorothy in the Wizard of Oz discovering it was all hokus pokus.

"I don't believe you!"

L. Frank Baum was cleverly pointing his finger at organized religion and calling it a humbug. Baum used the Wizard to communicate this conviction, man-made religion is an imposter, fraud, and deceiver. The Wizard remorsefully confessed to Dorothy, "I'm a humbug." The Wizard also represents a diabolical spirit within a person that manipulates, tricks, and deceives individuals. This will be explained later in the book.

Dorothy asked Glenda to help her go back home to Kansas. This scene stands out and captures the universal truth conveyed in this book.

You've always had the Power, my Dear.
You just had to learn it for yourself."
— Glenda the Good Witch

Glenda told Dorothy that she had the power to go home all along. Dorothy did not need a man-made religion and she did not have to say the "sinner's prayer" to go back to Kansas. The Power to go home was within her all the time, but she had to learn it for herself.

Dorothy learned a valuable lesson on the Yellow Brick Road. Baum used "backyard" as a metaphor for "within." Dorothy needed to look within herself and not outside of herself for spiritual wisdom and truth to go home. Gnostics called this "knowledge" or gnosis. The "truth" set her free and allowed her to return "home."

"If I ever go looking for my heart's desire again, I won't look any further than *my own backyard*. Because if it isn't there, I never lost it to begin with" Is that right?" Dorothy (backyard refers to her going within herself)

Dorothy then asked Glenda why she had never told her this before. The answer is brilliant because it applies to every soul… you just have to learn it for yourself.

> "You always had the power, my dear;
> *you just had to learn it yourself."*
> Glenda

In the first Matrix movie, Morpheus told Neo the same thing.

> *"Unfortunately, no one can be told what the Matrix is.*
> *You have to see it for yourself."*
> *Morpheus*

When Dorothy returned to Kansas and woke up in her bed, Aunt Em told her that she was just having a "dream." This is important and will be explained later in the book.

Plato's Allegory of the Cave

The Greek philosopher, Plato, wrote The Allegory of the Cave around 380 BCE. It is recognized as one of the greatest philosophical works in all classical literature. The Latin word for allegory is *allegoria,* a story, picture, or poem that can be interpreted to reveal a hidden meaning. The allegory is a short dialogue between Socrates (Plato's teacher) and Glaucon (Plato's older brother.) The dialogue uses layers of symbolism to communicate Plato's observation about the condition of humanity. Philosophers and scholars have interpreted the allegory in countless ways.

Ancient Mystery Schools

A mystery school is a brotherhood of initiates dedicated to learning about the soul's esoteric mysteries. We know about the existence of ancient mystery schools, but no one knows exactly what the students were taught. The sacred wisdom and higher knowledge imparted to the initiates were never revealed to the outside world because the members were sworn to secrecy.

Many scholars believe that Plato was a member of a sacred mystery school. This is a strong possibility if one links Plato to the ancient mystery schools that flourished in Greece, Rome, Egypt, and other parts of the ancient world. Many believe that Plato spent several years in Egypt studying esoteric truths in the mystery schools. About eleven miles from Athens was one of the ancient world's largest and most famous mystery schools. Because the Eleusinian Mystery School was in Plato's backyard, one can confidently speculate that he was an initiate and active member of this secret brotherhood.

Because religion was central to Greek life and culture, one can imagine how the mystery schools' ideas, beliefs, and esoteric knowledge influenced the great philosophers. The ancient temples with huge ornate columns and beautiful interiors fashioned in marble are artifacts of these magnificent temples. They give modern society a glimpse into the Greco, Egyptian, and Roman mindset, and how they valued their religious beliefs. The statutes of the deities, the rituals, and the pagan myths took on a deeper esoteric wisdom to the initiates of the mystery school.

They learned about the higher truths hidden from everyone on the outside. Those on the outside could not understand the rituals or stories and discarded them as foolishness. Only the initiates and members of the mystery schools understood the esoteric or hidden meanings in the rites, rituals, and myths. Members were required to take an oath and swear absolute secrecy. They promised to remain silent and not share their knowledge with anyone.

In modern times, the Freemasons are the closest fraternity that resembles the ancient mystery schools. Their brotherhood has existed for hundreds of years and is considered the oldest fraternal organization in the world. It is a secret fraternity of men initiated into rites of passage or degrees.

Their teachings are figurative, symbolic, and disguised in rituals that only members and initiates can understand. Much of the ancient Egyptian, Greek, and Roman mysteries are reproduced in modern Freemasonry. The walls of their "temples" are covered with Egyptian artwork. The "single eye," or the "All Seeing Eye," is one of the iconic symbols in Freemasonry. The list of members connected to Freemasonry is quite noteworthy. George Washington,

Benjamin Franklin, James Monroe, Thomas Jefferson, Winston Churchill, Voltaire, and Franklin D Roosevelt are just a few.

One can argue that Plato was writing The Allegory of the Cave to initiates of the Greek mystery schools who understood the hidden meaning of his allegories. They would view the dialogue as a spiritual teaching about the soul's ascension from spiritual bondage, blindness, and ignorance to illumination and enlightenment. (He was also writing about something else. That will be discussed later in the book.) Those outside the sacred mysteries might think that Plato was writing about philosophy, education, politics, and abstract forms. Manly Hall wrote, "Plato, an initiate of one of these sacred orders, was severely criticized because in his writings he revealed to the public many of the secret philosophic principles of the Mysteries." (The Secret Teachings of All Ages, Manly P Hall, page 40)

Socrates was a student of Plato and one of the main characters in The Allegory of the Cave. He is well known for his philosophy and axiom, "Know Thyself." These two words were carved on the top of the door at the temple of Delphi to remind mankind to contemplate one's true reality as spiritual beings having an earthly existence. This is a universal truism that transcends all religious thought. The Gospel of Thomas tells us, "When you come to know yourselves, then you will be known, and you will realize it is you who are the sons of the living Father." When an individual escapes the cave, one will experience a spiritual awakening, realization, and "knowing" that the words of Thomas are true.

The Allegory of the Cave is based on a delusion that reveals how humans incorrectly perceive reality. Here is a summary of the allegory. The setting is a dark cave with one opening located at the top of a steep ascent to the outside.

We are the prisoners in the cave.

There are prisoners chained to a wall since childhood who can only see moving shadows in the front of the cave. Behind the wall are puppeteers walking across an elevated walkway holding figures of animals and other objects. Behind the puppeteers is a large fire that casts shadows of the figures onto the cave's wall in front of the prisoners.

Because the prisoners only saw the shadows since childhood, they truly believed the shadows on the wall were real. One day a prisoner escaped and managed to make a very difficult ascent to the light coming through the opening in the cave. Because his eyes did not immediately adjust to the blinding light, he saw blurred images that looked different from the shadows in the cave. Eventually, his eyes adjusted, and he saw amazing colors and objects. He later gazed at a brilliant light that illuminated everything before him. The prisoner soon realized that the shadows in the cave he had looked at since childhood were not real. He painfully admitted to himself that they were just shadows. Because the prisoner escaped the cave, he discovered something much better and more real.

The prisoner soon realized he needed to share his experience with the other prisoners still chained to the wall in the cave. He returned to the dark cave and descended to the lower level, where the prisoners gazed at the shadows. Because of the drastic change from brilliant light to utter darkness, the prisoner's eyes did not adjust. His eyes hurt, and he could barely see in the cave's darkness. The prisoner eventually found his way to the other prisoners chained to the wall. He told them about his escape, finding the opening to the cave, the colors, objects, and the brilliant light. He tried to tell them that they were looking at shadows and were just false images appearing real.

The prisoners chained to the wall and looking at the shadows refused to listen to him and would not leave. The chained prisoners were so bothered and upset with the escaped prisoner that they wished it were possible to harm him, shut him up, and even kill him.

Allegory has many layers of hidden meanings, and one is free to consider countless possibilities. We can only speculate about Plato's true intentions and never know the answer. One could narrow down some of the choices by asking ourselves if he was speaking as a secular philosopher or as a Greek mystery school member writing about higher spiritual truths.

If Plato was writing as a member of a Greek mystery school, the initiated members would understand that he was talking about the ascent of the soul. The cave would represent spiritual darkness or a lower state of consciousness. The prisoners represent the unawakened souls of humanity who have been shackled in bondage to a wall of delusional thinking since childhood. The puppeteers are the deceivers, tricksters, and manipulators that perpetuate hokus pokus and the delusion of the shadows. The puppeteers use lies and hokus pokus to perpetuate the delusion. They hold up their dogmas, creeds, and man-made religion to cast shadows that misrepresent the truth and keep unawakened souls in bondage. The shadows represent the false evidence appearing real. Because the unawakened souls trusted their eyes to see the deceiving shadows and their hearing to listen to the manipulative sounds and words, they believed the shadows were real. The unawakened souls were chained in bondage to the wall of delusional thinking and could not escape. Although the shadows are a delusion, the unawakened souls are convinced the images are real and true. This is similar to the counterfeit spirit that will be explained later in the book.

The prisoner who escaped the bondage made a difficult climb out of the cave. It was like an "initiation" in a mystery school that revealed hidden truths. This is the ascent of the soul moving from spiritual darkness to the illumination of the higher truth. The climb upward and out of the cave is difficult. The bright light represents spiritual enlightenment that comes from within a person. After the inner light opened the prisoner's spiritual eyes, he wanted to share the "good news" with the other prisoners in bondage to the wall. Ultimately, the reader learns that unawakened souls do not want to hear this foolishness and resist the messenger. They prefer the comfort of the dark cave and choose not to leave.

The Shadows

The prisoners who were chained to the wall perceived the shadows as real. The shadows were images of the false evidence appearing real. Because man-made religion keeps unawakened souls in bondage through literalism and blind faith, individuals are prevented from seeing their true reality. Literalism is like the "shadow" in the cave because it is not real. Blind faith is the ultimate decoy that perpetuates delusional thinking. This deception prevents one from understanding the hidden metaphorical messages.

The ancient mystics and members of mystery schools never intended for anyone to take the stories and myths literally. Waking up removes the veil of literalism and reveals the esoteric truth hidden within the allegories, metaphors, and symbolisms. The cognitive delusion tricks or mocks the brain into believing the literal interpretation of the Bible is the absolute truth despite a lack of credible evidence, historical facts, and critical thinking. When the gospels were written almost two thousand years ago, citizens of the ancient world heard stories or attended drama plays as a rite of passage into an initiation into a higher degree of esoteric knowledge. They understood the stories were allegorical and should not be taken literally.

Plato's Fake Reality

Plato also used the shadows as a metaphor for this world's fake reality, illusion, and false reality. As a philosopher, Plato believed that only the spiritual realm or the Good God was real. The shadows represent the illusion, fake or false reality. This will be discussed in greater detail later in the book.

Coming Out of the Cave

Clouds are made of tiny water drops or ice crystals floating in the sky. Airplanes fly through them without any problem. But a small cloud can easily block the sun's brilliant light, warming heat, and life-sustaining energy. The false man-made religious system is like the small cloud that blocks the brilliant light of the True God from the hearts and minds of humanity.

The faith deconstruction movement is like coming out of a cave. Plato described this journey as a steep ascent. It isn't easy because you are learning and seeing things for the first time. The Gospel of Thomas encourages one to "continue seeking until he finds."

The Gospel of Thomas

"Let him who seeks continue seeking until he finds.

When he finds it, he will become troubled.

When he becomes troubled, he will be astonished,

and he will rule over the All."

Jesus said, "If those who lead you say to you, 'See, the kingdom is in the sky,' then the birds of the sky will precede you.

If they say to you, 'It is in the sea,' then the fish will precede you.

Rather, the kingdom is inside of you, and it is outside of you.

When you come to know yourselves, then you will become known, and you will realize that it is you who are the sons of the living father.

But if you will not know yourselves, you dwell in poverty, and it is you who are that poverty."

Spiritual Lessons from Gnostic Movies

In 1999 the Matrix captivated the public as an action-packed sci-fi movie. Most viewers applauded the film as science fiction. But a smaller audience saw something different and recognized the hidden messages, symbolisms, and spiritual overtones. The multi-layers of thought-provoking scenes are still topics of discussion. Many years later, images of red and blue pills are iconic symbols for truth seekers.

Individuals often use the word "matrix" to communicate a system of mind control that dominates our personal, political, ideological, and spiritual lives. While Neo is still sleeping at his desk, the computer starts typing… "Wake up Neo…. The Matrix has you." The image of him sleeping is especially important because it symbolizes a deeper meaning. He is oblivious to the subtle and manipulative methods used by the Matrix to control his mind. He is unconscious and unaware of the delusional thinking and hokus pokus that is keeping him in a dream state.

In ancient times, sleeping was a symbol of ignorance and spiritual death. The movie uses contemporary imagery to communicate similar ideas written in the Bible, fairy tales, and Hollywood movies.

Matrix

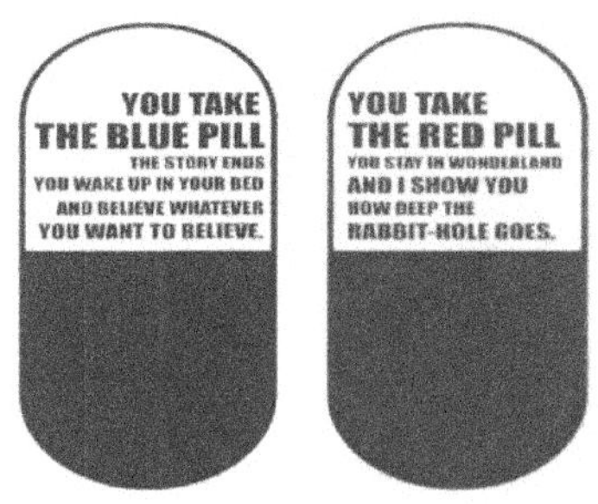

Morpheus offers Neo a choice between red and blue pills in the movie. Metaphorically taking the red pill symbolizes one's desire to learn life-changing truths, even if they do not agree with one's current convictions. Taking the blue pill represents the willingness to remain in blissful ignorance and continue to live in the Matrix.

The only way to escape the mental bondage of the Matrix is to metaphorically take the red pill and obtain gnosis and Divine knowledge. Man-made religion hands out the blue pill every Sunday which encourages members of the congregation to believe delusional thinking and hokus pokus.

"Neo:

Why do my eyes hurt?

Morpheus: You've never used them before.

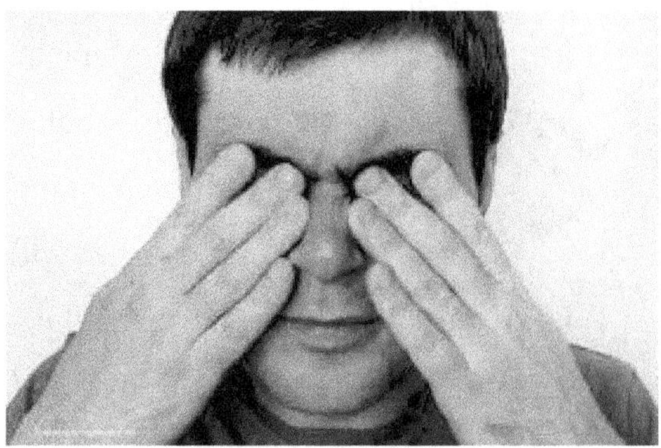

MORPHEUS

The Matrix is everywhere, it's all around us, here even in this room. You can see it out your window or on your television. You feel it when you go to work or go to church or pay your taxes. *It is the world that has been pulled over your eyes to blind you from the truth.*

NEO

What truth?

MORPHEUS

That you are a slave, Neo. That you, like everyone else, was born into bondage.... kept inside a prison that you cannot smell, taste, or touch. *A prison for your mind.*

MORPHEUS

Unfortunately, no one can be told what the Matrix is. *You have to see it for yourself.*

MORPHEUS

You take the blue pill, and the story ends. You wake up in your bed, and you believe whatever you want to believe.

You take the red pill, and you stay in Wonderland, and I show you how deep the rabbit-hole goes.

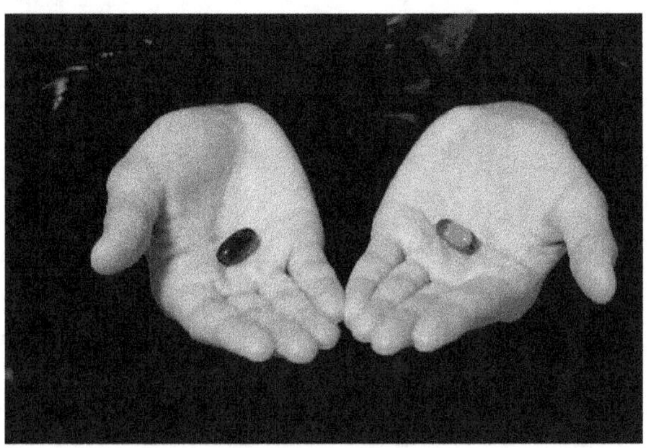

Morpheus

Remember that all I am offering is the truth.... nothing more.

Morpheus warned Neo that by taking the red pill, he would show him how deep down the rabbit hole goes… and that all he was offering was the truth. The "red pill" opens your eyes, and you begin to see things from a new perspective. One is empowered to disregard group thinking and question everything the "Matrix" uses to blind humanity from the truth. The "red pill" is a metaphor for waking up to the truth and escaping the bondage of the cave.

Spiritual Lessons from Fairy Tales

We will leave The Wizard of OZ and visit another example of contemporary literature that uses symbolism, metaphors, and hidden meanings to convey a hidden meaning.

"Once upon a time" is the traditional way to begin a fairy tale. For decades, readers would read these four words and immediately know that the story is unreal. It was understood that the princess, prince, and evil stepmother were not real people. These stories are filled with fictional characters and places that stretch one's imagination. Despite the dark and mysterious plots that often make no sense to the average reader, fairy tales have captivated children's and adults' minds for hundreds of years.

There is something intrinsically special about fairy tales that allow them to transcend time. Helen Blavatsky was a mystic and co-founder founder of the Theosophy Society. (Frank Baum and the Wonderful Wizard of Oz) She was recognized worldwide as one of the greatest esoteric thinkers of her generation. She talked about fairy tales and wrote that there is an audience who "are the few real seekers in any generation of humanity — those who recognize that fairy tales have an inner meaning, a meaning about what goes on inside us, within our minds and psyches. They know that every real fairy tale is a story we experience in the depths of our being." (Theosophy World Resource Center, Fairy Tales)

Their universal popularity has carried over into several blockbuster movies, college courses, and hundreds of books. When an individual only thinks about fairy tales as children's stories, one misses the story's hidden moral and spiritual treasures. Most characters in fairy tales do not have traditional names because they represent you and me.

Fairy Tales Are About Us

If the reader looks in a mirror, one will see the hero in every fairy tale. Each character has a specific role to play. Witches may represent the dark side of ourselves or aspects that we have repressed. A big bad wolf appears in fairy tales like Little Red Riding Hood, Three Little Pigs, and the Wolf in Sheep's Clothing. The wolf is an antagonist and a trickster who wants to seduce or kill you. The forest ("wilderness or desert in the Bible) is the location of our unconscious aspects of ourselves. The forest is usually dark and the home of scary animals and creepy things. The hero (you) often gets lost in the forest. Most often, the princess represents our soul in spiritual transformation or awakening. In the Greek myth Psyche and Eros (Cupid), the lesson was obvious to the people listening to the tale. The name of the main character who fell asleep was Psyche; her name means "soul" in Greek. The evil stepmother represents the ego, carnal mind, or man-made religion that wants to keep the soul in bondage. The hidden wisdom of the fairy tale reveals that all the characters are inside us. They represent the masculine, feminine, heart, soul, intellect, and emotions within us.

Prominent psychologists like Sigmund Freud and Carl Jung discovered the universal wisdom and practical applications of fairy tales and applied their findings to the dynamics of the unconscious mind and human behavior. The science of psychology uses myth and fairy tales to unlock the psychodramas or chaos that unfolds within the human mind. Carl Jung, a world-famous psychologist, is well known for his writings on fairy tales and the human psyche. He interpreted the dominant themes and characters and applied them to universal principles or archetypes of the human persona. His brilliant work removed the common belief that fairy tales are merely children's stories. Marie von Franz collaborated with Carl Jung and pioneered a study of fairy tales and their relationship to the human psyche. She wrote more than twenty books on fairy tales.

More importantly, fairy tales also provide spiritual lessons about our soul's journey or transition from spiritually sleeping to waking up and escaping the bondage that has chained us to the false shadows of delusion and the false evidence appearing real. Adults often dismiss fairy tales and push them on to their children as bedtime stories. If a parent wanted to purchase a book about Cinderella, Snow White, or Sleeping Beauty at a local bookstore, the salesclerk would point the customer to the children's section. On the contrary, fairy tales were written for adults but disguised in children's clothing.

Fairy tales are hundreds of years old and primarily written for an adult audience. The earliest fairy tales were often dark, gruesome, morbid, and sexual. Each one has been modified and recreated to fit the culture and ethnicity of the country. For example, the same story may feature a French, German, Chinese, or American theme. Storytellers orally handed them down and later wrote them down. These fictional stories were meant for adults to reveal the truth about our human condition. They are like "parables" because they are usually short fictitious stories illustrating a moral attitude or a religious principle.

Fairy tales hide their true message in symbolism, metaphors, and allegories. Often the esoteric or hidden messages have a spiritual message. The princess, handsome prince, evil stepmother, witches, and various animals are symbols that represent the dynamics that occur within a person as the soul awakens and transitions from its lower nature into its higher nature. It is like the metamorphosis of a caterpillar into a beautiful butterfly. At the end of the story, good wins and evil is defeated, the prince rescues the young lady, and the main characters live "happily ever after."

Before fairy tales, the world used mythology to communicate these universal truths. Horus, Apollo, Zeus, Isis, Osiris, and Hercules are just a few mythological characters or deities that symbolized hidden spiritual truths in the ancient world. Mythology and fairy tales were understood as non-literal and correctly understood as symbolic.

The storyline and plot convey a profound message when a

person mindfully reflects on a fairy tale and identifies the underlying symbolisms. It becomes even more meaningful when you relate the fairy tale to the "things" inside your mind. Often the underlying message portrays the journey of the soul from "spiritual sleeping" to "enlightenment" or ascending from "lower consciousness" to "higher consciousness." Nature uses the metamorphosis of a caterpillar into a beautiful butterfly teaches this lesson. The stages are egg, caterpillar, chrysalis, and adult. The soul's journey is disguised in characters going through trials and tribulations, often tormented by an evil stepmother or a scary animal.

Fairy tales often communicate a universal truth that the soul is "sleeping." The theme of "sleeping" is an important part of the storyline in Sleeping Beauty, Snow White, Rip VanWinke, and other fairy tales. Because the story's theme is wrapped in symbolism, it is necessary to think outside of the literal words and images of the fairy tale. Sleeping Beauty, Snow White, and Rip Van Winkle were not physically sleeping. "Sleeping" in the story represents a state of mind. The fictional characters represent the unawakened soul that is spiritually sleeping.

Fairy tales often have spiritual overtones. Characters in fairy tales falling into a deep sleep symbolize a spiritual sleep or spiritual ignorance to them. When one takes a deep dive into the murky waters of "faith deconstruction," one discovers the reality of spiritually sleeping. Most Christians are "spiritually sleepwalking" and living in a cave chained to a wall of fear and ignorance. (Plato's Allegory of the Cave) The delusion of lies and the false evidence appearing real keep individuals in this mental prison of spiritual darkness and bondage.

An optometrist refers to a "blind spot" as a scotoma. It is a physical defect in the eye that prevents external objects from being seen. Spiritual "blind spots" are cognitive or delusional impairments that prevent individuals from understanding something, despite the overwhelming evidence to the contrary. The mystical Christ, or the inner voice within, said," I have come into the world to give sight to those who are blind and to show those who think they see that they are blind." John 9:39

Hokus Pokus

A Practical Guide to Deconstruction

There is a quote on the internet, without a source, which is often used to convey the message that most people are asleep....so true.

1% Control the World

4% Are Sell Out Puppets

90% Are Asleep

5% Know and are trying to wake the 90% up

The 1% Don't want the 5% to wake up the 90%.

Snow White

This is a brief description of the fairy tale of Snow White and the Seven Dwarfs. The evil queen disguised herself as a farmer's wife and offered Snow White a poisoned apple. (Sound familiar?) She gives the red poisoned apple to Snow White; the girl eagerly takes a bite and then falls into a deep coma appearing to be dead. The evil queen thought she finally triumphed and killed Snow White. Because the seven dwarfs could not revive Snow White, they placed her in a glass

casket. She remained in the casket for a long time until a prince appeared. The prince kisses Snow White, and she wakes up. This symbolizes a magical divine kiss, or gnosis and Divine knowledge, which breathes new life into the sleeping soul. Can you see the spiritual overtones of Snow White spiritually sleeping and waking up by a divine kiss?

Sleeping Beauty

In a nutshell, Sleeping Beauty pricked her finger on a spindle. She fell onto an old blanket on the attic floor and fell into a deep sleep. Everyone in the castle, servants, and royals, all fell asleep. Even the prince, still waiting for her outside the tower, fell asleep. Within hours, thorns and vines sprung up and wrapped around the castle. The vegetation was so thick that no human or beast could pass through. In the original story, Sleeping Beauty sleeps for one hundred years before the prince's kiss awakens her. The prince represents gnosis, Divine truth, and wisdom that wakes Sleeping Beauty from her spiritual coma.

Cinderella

Cinderella is one of the most beloved fairy tales of all time. It is about us. The story begins when her mother died. This is a common theme in fairy tales and the hero is on a journey to self-awareness or individualization.

She is a young woman who is mistreated and verbally abused by her cruel stepmother and jealous stepsisters. Cinderella was put into servitude doing menial chores day and night. Fairy tales are like allegories that use fictional characters to illustrate a moral lesson or spiritual truth. The cruel stepmother represents the archetype of any person or institution that makes a person think less of themselves. For example, man-made religion can manipulate individuals through fearmongering, condemnation, and hokus pokus to make a person feel sinful, guilty, fearful, and inadequate.

In the fairy tale there was a ball, and the cruel stepmother did not allow Cinderella to go. The day of the ball arrived, and Cinderella was left alone at the house wishing she could go. A fairy god mother appeared and encouraged Cinderella to go to the ball. The fairy god mother used her magic wand to create six magnificent horses, a beautiful carriage, a coachman, and a beautiful gown with glass slippers. Cinderella met a prince at the ball, and they fell in love. They were married and lived happily ever after.

The story about Cinderella is about the experience of one's soul trapped in a mental prison of inferiority, separation, fear, guilt, and condemnation. We witness a transformation in Cinderella as she progresses from a lowly servant to a princess. This is symbolic of the ascension of the soul when a person spiritually awakens, and the lower consciousness grows into a higher consciousness. She was rescued by a charming prince (gnosis) and restored to her natural state of perfection and wholeness through a sacred marriage.

Hansel and Gretel

The story of Hansel and Gretel is a tale that originated in Germany between 1250 and 1500. Modern versions were adapted by the Brothers Grimm around 1850. Because fairy tales are esoteric and symbolic, the higher wisdom is hidden. Exploring Hansel and Gretel and taking a deep dive below the surface of the children's story will be helpful. Because fairy tales are subjective and not dogmatic, there is no right or wrong interpretation. What does the fairy tale Hansel and Gretel mean to you?

The tale of Hansel and Gretel is like a comingling of the stories of Adam and Eve, the prodigal son, and the Wizard of Oz. Hansel is a masculine name of Scandinavian, German, and Hebrew origins. It means God is gracious. The name Gretel means Pearl. Jesus of Nazareth spoke of the "pearl of great price" as a metaphor for the kingdom of heaven. Their names give us clues that the fairy tale about Hansel and Gretel is talking about spiritual things.

The woodcutter and the stepmother sent Hansel and Gretel into the forest. This is like the story of Adam and Eve. "So the LORD God sent them out of the Garden of Eden and made them cultivate the soil from which they had been formed." Gen 3: 23 Hansel and Gretel are the heroes of the story. They represent you and me, the duality of our masculine and feminine nature, and the soul. When the soul is sent out from its spiritual home, it incarnates into a physical body. It soon becomes lost in the "forest" of life or the "distant country" like the prodigal son. There are strange, mysterious things, darkness, chaos, and even a wicked witch. Hansel and Gretel walked a path just like the "Yellow Brick Road." Their spiritual path led them to an awakening. Because this is a universal truth, the theme shows up over and over again in stories like the prodigal son returning to his spiritual home, and Dorothy finding her way back to Kansas.

They saw a "pretty snow-white bird" sitting on a bough on the way, so they followed him. The bird flew to a house made of bread, cake, and sugar. It is commonly referred to as a gingerbread or candy house. On the surface, the "snow white bird" looks like God is leading Hansel and Gretel to a safe place. The young souls believed they made the right decision because the house was made of bread, cake, and sugar. They were famished for something to eat. It turns out that the "pretty snow-white bird" deceived them and led them to an evil witch. This is the counterfeit spirit that copies the

True spirit and deceives humanity. The lesson of the snow-white bird" is the same lesson that Dorothy learned in the Wizard of Oz. "If I ever go looking for my heart's desire again, I won't look any further than my own backyard. Because if it isn't there, I never lost it to begin with" Is that right?" The pretty "snow-white bird" was sitting on a bough outside of Hansel and Gretel; they were not looking in their own "backyard" or within themselves to hear the voice of God.

Hansel and Gretel were greeted by an old woman leaning on a crutch. She took them by the hand and led them into her house. Although the old woman was "so kind," she built the little house to entice and kill them. One can imagine that the "gingerbread house" represents a variety of meaningful deceptions.

To remain consistent with the theme of this book, the gingerbread house" is the delusion, lies, and hokus pokus of man-made religion. The candy is the promise of going to heaven and escaping eternal punishment if one belongs to this "gingerbread house." Music and entertainment are part of the gingerbread house. The emotional music is like "spiritual candy" tricking people into believing their "emotional high" is a spiritual experience. The "worship" team stirs up the emotions in the congregation and tricks individuals into believing that the modern-day "gingerbread house" is a holy place or a house of God. This is an example of the counterfeit spirit that will be discussed later in the book.

Hansel and Gretel came to their senses, just like the prodigal son and Dorothy in the Wizard of Oz. They all killed the wicked "witch." When Dorothy came to her senses, she told the Wizard he was lying. When Hansel and Gretel came to their senses, they pushed the wicked witch into the oven. At the end of the fairy tale, Hansel and Gretel rejoiced and danced because "they had nothing more to fear." They also discovered chests of pearls and precious stones.

They returned to their (spiritual) home and embraced their Father just like the prodigal son. The lesson learned by Hansel and Gretel in the "gingerbread house" is extremely important, the wicked witch is out to spiritually kill us.

Bible Stories

Jonah

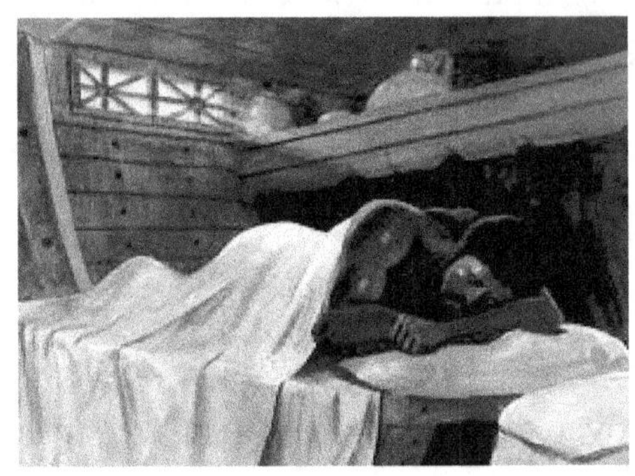

The story of Jonah and the whale is not a literal account of a man swallowed by a huge fish. Unfortunately, many adults and children still believe the Bible is written about a historical event that really happened. The man-made religion has indoctrinated unawakened souls into believing literal stories and continues to perpetuate the delusion in children's Bible classes. The unawakened soul follows the blind guides… hook, line, and sinker. The story of Jonah is a spiritual allegory filled with deep hidden truths. It begins by telling the reader that Jonah was in the lowest parts of the ship, i.e., in deep spiritual darkness and was fast asleep or spiritually dead.

Samson

The story of Samson and Delilah is a popular Bible story that is most often taken literally and taught to children who are not mature enough to question the absurd narrative. Many adults still believe that Samson had supernatural strength, killed a lion with his bare hands, and killed an entire army of Philistines with a jawbone. They also believe that Samson pushed the stone pillars of the temple apart with his bare hands. The picture of Samson sleeping enhances our understanding of the meaning of "sleeping" in the Bible. The story of Samson never happened; the authors used the characters of Samson and Delilah to communicate a spiritual allegory. Delilah represents the lower emotions tricking the higher self into a deep sleep and taking his strength away.

"And she made him sleep upon her knees, and she called for a man, and she caused him to shave off the seven locks of his head, and she began to afflict him, and his strength went from him." Judges 6:19

"Awake, you who sleep,

arise from the dead,"

Eph 5:14

Gnostic Paul was not writing to physically dead cadavers and urging them to wake up. He was figuratively writing to unawakened souls. Separating the literal from the non-literal is crucial to waking up. Because the spiritually unawakened souls are trapped in bondage to the delusion of literalism, a veil covers the allegories, symbolisms, and hidden meanings in the Bible. Paul compared literalism to milk and the non-literal allegories to solid food.

In medical terminology, Egersis is an extreme state of alert wakefulness, often used in the context of insomnia. This Greek word

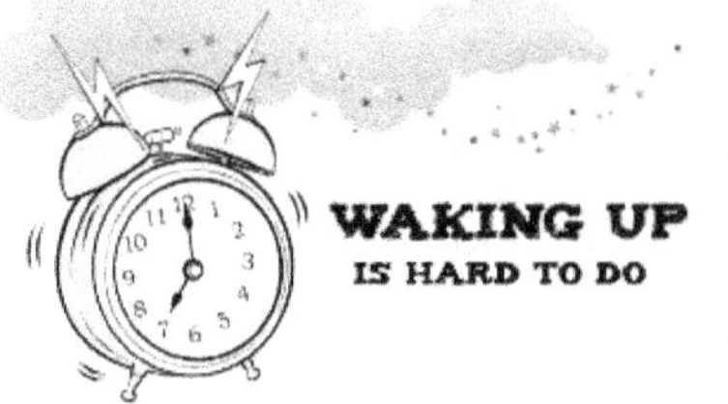

is usually translated as a rousing up, a rising, and an excitation. In Christian theology, it's a stand-in for "Resurrection." (Wikipedia) The original Greek word "egersis" is translated as a rousing up or awakening. The influence of Christianity did a hokus pokus and changed the correct interpretation of the word. According to Strong's G1454, "egersis" is a rousing excitation, a rising, and a resurrection from the dead. In the minds of ancient Greek thought, "dead" referred to the soul.

Through gnosis or knowledge, the spiritually dead soul awakens and is resurrected.

Awakening = Gnosis and Resurrection of the Soul

Waking up is hard because the mainstream church does not want its members to wake up to the "things" that Jesus taught in the Gospels. They have placed mental roadblocks of fear and eternal punishment to prevent people from looking outside the walls of their dogma and doctrines.

SNOOZE

Hokus Pokus

Definition of hokus pokus:
1: *Sleight of hand*
2: *nonsense or sham used especially to cloak deception*
Merriam-Webster Dictionary

Magicians often use these words before they pull a rabbit out of the hat or perform other illusionary tricks. Another word often used by magicians is abracadabra. It appears that a magician has a secret power when he uses these words. He can make impossible things happen by saying "hokus pokus" or "abracadabra." This is like our previous discussion of delusion and F.E.A.R. or the false evidence appearing real. Both create a deception.

In Christianity, there is a communion service that both Catholics and Protestants use in their services. Both use bread or crackers and wine or grape juice to represent the body and blood of Jesus. In the Protestant tradition, the bread and wine are merely symbols. However, Catholicism believes in transubstantiation or a supernatural transformation of the bread and wine into the actual body and blood of Jesus. When the priest says, "This is my body" and "This is my blood," a supernatural miracle happens, and the earthly substances of bread and wine are transfigured and changed into the actual body and blood of Jesus of Nazareth.

Hundreds of years ago, priests used Latin in the Mass. When he raised the host, he would say, "Hoc est Corpus." Because the common folk could not speak or understand Latin, the Latin phrase was often mistranslated into hokus pokus. No one knows if this story is fact or fiction, but the implication is far-reaching and something for Catholics to think about.

One does not need to say "hokus pokus" or "abracadabra" to create deception. In the modern world, people are familiar with the term "fake news." It is so widely accepted that the words have been added to modern dictionaries. *Fake news* conveys or incorporates false, fabricated, or deliberately misleading information. Most Americans recognize "fake news" as false, deceptive, and a distortion of the truth. It is fabricated and often made up without verifiable facts or credible sources. This raises the question, why are so many people vulnerable to the lies and false information of the media? Are people simply gullible and naïve? Do people lack the intelligence to separate a false belief from verifiable evidence? Because F.E.A.R. or the false evidence appearing real is like a wolf in sheep's clothing, one needs to set a mental truth alarm that shouts, "This is hokus pokus."

One might think that "fake news" just started recently and did not exist before 2016. Lies, deception, and misinformation have been around throughout history. Although most people are open to the idea that the news media cannot be trusted, they are not open and adamantly resist the suggestion that their church cannot be trusted.

Like the "fake news," religion is also guilty of lies, deception, and a distortion of the truth. Hundreds of years ago, the Roman Church used forgeries and deliberately mistranslated crucial verses in the New Testament to alter the sacred texts' original meaning to perpetuate the Roman Church's literal theology. Scholars have suggested that between eight and eleven of the twenty-seven books of the New Testament are forgeries. Many skeptics, scholars, and theologians suggest the gospels were copied from pagan myths.

The counterfeit spirit hijacked the truth and turned it into hokus pokus. Billions of people throughout the world have been deceived by the Father of Lies into believing the "shadows" are real. Plato's Allegory of the Cave is a visual illustration of prisoners chained in bondage since childhood believing the shadows on the wall are real.

Reinventing God

This topic is important for anyone who is deconstructing because it asks the foundational question about God. After the scribes did a hokus pokus, abracadabra and changed the name of Yahweh to Lord, few Bible readers take the time to deconstruct this "holy" name. Because this information has been suppressed for hundreds of years, the proper identity and origins of Yahweh have escaped public awareness. When the scribes translated the Bible, they changed the holy name to "Lord" so the reader would not have to pronounce it. It also hid the name and prevented truth seekers from looking into the true origins of this *pagan* deity. In modern times religious Jews still believe the name Yahweh is so sacred and holy they will not speak it aloud.

Both Judaism and Christianity share the same God who is omnipotent and the creator of heaven and earth. His name is Yahweh or the word derivative Jehovah. Both Jews and Christians pray to Him, worship Him, and obey Him. Although modern day believers believe the "Lord" of the Old Testament is God Almighty, many of the earliest Christians rejected this idea. The Gnostic Gospels write about this in great detail. Both Jesus of Nazareth and Gnostic Paul taught their disciples that Yahweh is not the True God. The church covers this up with delusional thinking and hokus pokus.

Hokus Pokus
A Practical Guide to Deconstruction

When a person studies the Bible using critical thinking, reason, and common sense, the truth-seeker discovers two separate and distinct Gods in the Bible. There is a jealous, angry, psychopathic god in the Old Testament and a loving God, Abba Father, in the New Testament. Man-made religion perpetuates the hokus pokus and delusional thinking that these two deities are the same. Jesus of Nazareth was sent to humanity to reveal his loving Father and teach people that the True God is not Yahweh.

In the Matrix Movie, the "blue pill" is a metaphor for blind faith, simple beliefs, and a lack of critical thinking. "You take the blue pill, the story ends. You wake up in your bed and *believe whatever you want to.*" Because most of humanity chooses to take the blue pill, individuals believe whatever they want or *whatever they are told to believe.* Christians who believe the God of the Old Testament and the God of the New Testament are the same are deceived by the counterfeit spirit and the Father of Lies. If this is believable, the True God has a dissociative identity disorder.

(DID) or a multiple personality disorder. This is a mental illness that is sometimes called a split personality. There are two distinct sets of thoughts, actions, and behaviors that are completely different. Do you believe the True God has a split personality?

If you study ancient history, one will learn that the biblical Israelites did not believe in a single, universal god until much later. They had a pantheon of deities. The pantheon of gods included El, Yahweh, Baal, and Asherah. El was the supreme deity.

In the earliest Biblical literature Yahweh is a storm god and a warrior god; he was not God Almighty or the creator as Judaism and Christianity currently teach their members. Yahweh was a Canaanite storm god who created violent winds and rains.

Yahweh was also a bloodthirsty warrior god and destroyer who killed men, women, children, and animals. "Scholars generally contend that Yahweh emerged as a "divine warrior" associated first with Seir, Edom, Paran and Teman, and later with Canaan." (Wikipedia)

- The LORD is a **warrior,** the LORD is his name. Exodus 15:3

- The LORD will go forth like a **warrior**, He will arouse His zeal like **a man of war**. He will utter a shout, yes, He will raise a war cry. He will prevail against His enemies. Isaiah 42:13

- He breaks through me with breach after breach; He runs at me **like a warrior**. Job 16:14

The Old Testament describes Yahweh as evil, malevolent, sadistic, jealous, angry, arrogant, unforgiving, narcissistic, and a mass murderer. He ordered the genocide of millions of men, women, children, and animals. The Gnostics believed that Yahweh was a lower "deity" and not the True God who they named the Monad. They called Yahweh the Demiurge or god of this world.

The god El was considered the supreme deity or Almighty God of the Canaanites, and Yahweh was one of many subordinate gods during the Bronze Age. According to mythology each "child" of El was assigned a territory or region to look over; Baal ruled over Canaan and Yahweh was given Israel. Hundreds of years later, Yahweh assimilated many of the characteristics of El and eventually replaced El as the supreme deity in the Iron Age.

Hokus Pokus

A Practical Guide to Deconstruction

By His Fruits, You Shall Know Him

Earlier in this book it was suggested that the reader use this truth detector to arrive at the truth, "By their fruits, you shall know them." Using this truth detector, ask yourself if the bloodthirsty, serial killer Yahweh is the True God or an imposter.

- Now go, attack the Amalekites, and totally destroy all that belongs to them. Do not spare them; *put to death men and women, children* and infants, cattle and sheep, camels and donkeys. 1 Sam 15:3

- Now therefore *kill every male among the little ones and kill every woman* that hath known man by lying with him. But all the women children, that have not known a man by lying with him, keep alive for yourselves. Numbers 31:17-18

- Then the LORD *rained upon Sodom and upon Gomorrah brimstone* and fire from the LORD out of heaven; *And he overthrew those cities, and all the plain, and all the inhabitants of the cities, and that which grew upon the ground.* Gen 19 24-25

- And it came to pass, that at midnight the LORD *smote all the firstborn* in the land of Egypt, from the firstborn of Pharaoh that sat on his throne unto the firstborn of the captive that was in the dungeon, and all the firstborn of cattle. Exodus 12:29

- And God saw that the wickedness of man was great in the earth, and that every imagination of the thoughts of his heart was only evil continually. And it repented the LORD that he had made man on the earth, and it grieved him at his heart. And the LORD said, *I will destroy man whom I have created from the face of the earth; both man, and beast, and the creeping thing, and the fowls of the air;* for it repenteth me that I have made them. Gen 6 5-7

- Also in Horeb ye provoked the LORD to wrath, so that the LORD was *angry with you* to have destroyed you. Deut 9:8

- In the greatness of your majesty you threw down those who opposed you. You unleashed your burning anger; it consumed them like stubble. Exodus 15:7

- The LORD your God is among you. He wants you to worship only him. If you worship other gods, God will be very angry with you. And he will destroy you from the face of the land. Deut 6:15

Christians believe in a God who condemns sinners to eternal torture and damnation for eternity. They ignore the teachings of Jesus of Nazareth and the truth contained in the parable of the Prodigal Son. The True God offers sinners unconditional love and forgiveness.

"But the father said to his servants, 'Bring quickly the best robe, and put it on him, and put a ring on his hand, and shoes on his feet. And bring the fattened calf and kill it and let us eat and celebrate. For this my son was dead, and is alive again; he was lost, and is found.' And they began to celebrate." Luke 15 22-24

By his fruits, Yahweh cannot be the True God. Man-made religion is teaching hokus pokus and delusional thinking to keep unawakened souls shackled in the cave. The counterfeit spirit and the Father of Lies has tricked humanity into believing a lie. Yahweh is an imposter or false god to keep unawakened souls from knowing the True God or Abba Father.

"I am the Lord your God" appears in the Bible over 150 times. Yahweh (Satan) is the Father of Lies deceiving humanity that he is the True God.

The Father of Lies tricks unawakened souls

into worshiping him.

"I, even I, am the LORD,

And besides Me there is no savior."

Is 43:11

Hokus Pokus
A Practical Guide to Deconstruction

All We Want Is Truth

"I'm sick and tired of hearing things from
Uptight short sided narrow minded hypocrites
All I want is the truth, just give me some truth."
John Lennon

It is time for man-made religion to *tell the truth about the True God.* The survival of humanity depends on unawakened souls waking up to the realization that the powers of darkness control our world. Every soul that wakes up weakens the power of the rulers of this world. Because man-made religion submits to the *"god of this world,"* humanity is inflicted with worldwide chaos, suffering, wars, disease, famine, and corruption.

Man-made religion teaches hokus pokus and delusional thinking about the evil god of the Old Testament. Jesus of Nazareth did not worship or pray to Yahweh; He rejected him as the counterfeit spirit who claimed to be the True God. Jesus of Nazareth was sent to reveal the True God and teach people Yahweh is an evil imposter.

Why does Christianity call Yahweh God when Jesus of Nazareth rejected him? Jesus of Nazareth was sent to reveal the True God, Abba Father, to humanity. He speaks to humanity when he said, "you do not know Him." Because Christianity worships the god of the Old Testament, Jesus of Nazareth would point to Christians and say *"Ye neither know me, nor my Father."*

- *You do not know Him,* but I know him because I am from him, and he sent me. John 7:29

- They will treat you this way because of my name, for *they do not know the one who sent me.* John 15:21

- Jesus answered, If I honour myself, my honour is nothing: it is my Father that honoureth me; of whom ye say, that he is your God: *Yet ye have not known him*; but I know him: and if I should say, I know him not, I shall be a liar like unto you: but I know him and keep his saying. Yet ye have not known him; but I know him: and if I should say, I know him not, I shall be a liar like unto you: but I know him and keep his saying. John 8 54-55

- Then said they unto him, Where is thy Father? Jesus answered, *Ye neither know me, nor my Father:* if ye had known me, ye should have known my Father also. John 8:19

- Ye are of *your father the devil*, and the lusts of your father ye will do. He was a murderer from the beginning, and abode not in the truth, because there is no truth in him. When he speaketh a lie, he speaketh of his own: for he is a liar, and the father of it. John 8:44

In the 1950's there was an extremely popular TV gameshow called To Tell the Truth. There were three contestants who stood in front of the camera and claimed to be the real person. The panelists were allowed to ask questions knowing that two of the contestants were imposters and were lying and pretending; they also knew that only one contestant was telling the truth. After time expired, the host would ask "Will the real (person's name) please stand up? It is time for Christians to ask *Will the True God please stand up.*

Will the True God please stand up.

1) God of the Old Testament who is a warrior and psychopath?

2) God of the New Testament who is a loving Abba Father?

3) God who has a split personality and is both evil and loving.

Hokus Pokus

Most Christians will incorrectly answer number 3 because that is what they have been taught for two thousand years. Yahweh has a split personality and is both a tyrant and a loving, merciful God.

The stories of the flood, Sodom and Gomorrah, and many other atrocities in the Old Testament give the truth seeker undeniable evidence that Yahweh cannot be the True God or the Father of Jesus of Nazareth. Yahweh is an evil bloodthirsty lower god of this world. Yahweh is the Father of Lies deceiving humanity and creating a counterfeit spirit to make himself appear to be "God Almighty." The shocking truth is very disturbing.

Christians are not worshiping the True God;

they worship the Father of Lies.

Yahweh will be discussed in greater detail later in the book with more detailed information that exposes the false god of this world from the True God. At this time, the reader only needs to consider the possibility that man-made religion reinvented Yahweh.

Reinventing The Trinity

The "doctrine of the Trinity is man-made hokus pokus and delusional thinking. Man-made religion has indoctrinated believers into thinking the Trinity was inspired by God and carved in stone like the Ten Commandments. It is not inspired nor was it carved in stone. The Christian version of the Trinity evolved over hundreds of years of intense debates and bitter feuds.

A doctrine that took the Church Fathers hundreds of years to establish must wave a red flag to truth seekers. It is hokus pokus.

Although the Trinity is not found in either of the books of the New Testament nor the Hebrew scriptures, the "church fathers reinvented the True God into three separate persons. They did a hokus pokus, abracadabra and changed One into three and then called it One. This concept is confusing and controversial. Because the average lay person cannot understand the theological gobbledygook, most unawakened souls pay little attention to this blasphemous doctrine and believe it hook, line, and sinker. It also proves the point of Occam's razor that something that is complicated is most often false.

"Neither the word "Trinity" nor the explicit doctrine appears in the New Testament, nor did Jesus and his followers intend to contradict the Shema in the Hebrew Scriptures: "Hear, O Israel: The Lord our God is one Lord" Deuteronomy 6:4 (Britannica)

Because the Trinity is the central doctrine of the Christian faith, there should be concrete evidence, beyond any doubt to support this claim. The doctrine of the Trinity must be a necessary subject for deconstruction. By using critical thinking and common sense, rather than blind faith, one will see the hokus pokus used by the Council of Nicaea and later by the Church Fathers to perpetuate this delusional thinking.   The definition of "monotheism" shared by other traditions is founded on the belief there is only *one* deity.

Church history shows a gradual assimilation of pagan ideas into Christianity. One of the most important was the trinity doctrine. It was formally introduced in 325 A.D. at the Council of Nicaea and later made official at the First Council of Constantinople in 381 A.D. The doctrine of the Trinity is a counterfeit spirit or a doctrine of demons that has deceived billions of unawakened souls for hundreds of years. The counterfeit spirit will be discussed in greater detail later in this book. It will explain in greater detail how truth was hijacked and replaced with a blasphemous doctrine that reinvented the True God is not three persons in one. The Hebrew Scriptures are correct in their understanding of monotheism…. "Hear, O Israel: The Lord Thy God is One Lord" Deut 6:4

The doctrine of the Trinity sets Christianity apart from other world religions. Church councils and church fathers sold this heresy to uneducated peasants by telling them they would go to hell if they did not believe it and bribing the nobility with all sorts of lavish benefits to recruit them. Because this doctrine has been indoctrinated into the minds of believers for nearly two thousand years, most Christians do not understand it and blindly accept it without giving it much thought.

The doctrine of the Trinity is man-made hokus pokus that was invented to support the political and religious goals of the Roman Church. It was codified in the Nicene Creed, Apostles' Creed, and the Athanasian Creed. All of them share belief in the three persons in one God.

Athanasius of Alexandria was a Christian theologian, a Church Father, and the chief defender of the Trinity. He spent many years defending his belief in the Trinity that was radically opposed by his Arian opponents who rejected the divinity of Jesus. After he died, he was called the "Pillar of the Church" and venerated as a saint. Although many believe the Creed was not written by

Athanasius, the Athanasian Creed is still valid and highly respected in the Catholic Church.

Here are portions of the Athanasian Creed

Whoever desires to be saved should above all hold to the catholic faith. Anyone who does not keep it whole and unbroken will doubtless perish eternally.

Now this is the catholic faith:

That we worship one God in trinity and the trinity in unity, neither blending their persons nor dividing their essence. For the person of the Father is a distinct person, the person of the Son is another, and that of the Holy Spirit still another. But the divinity of the Father, Son, and Holy Spirit is one, their glory equal, their majesty coeternal.

Now this is the true faith:

That we believe and confess that our Lord Jesus Christ, God's Son, is both God and human, equally. That we believe and confess that our Lord Jesus Christ, God's Son, is both God and human, equally.

Those who have done good will enter eternal life, and those who have done evil will enter eternal fire. *This is the catholic faith: one cannot be saved without believing it firmly and faithfully.*

(This is not an attack or judgement on the Catholic religion. It is above all discernment and awareness of the diabolical threats of eternal punishment and damnation used to spread hokus pokus.)

Reinventing The Mystical Jesus

Jesus of Nazareth asked Peter, "who do you say I am?" This question is not limited to Peter. Jesus is speaking to everyone. Have you answered this question for yourself…? *Who do you say I am?* It does not matter what your parents believed, and it certainly does not matter what the bishops believed hundreds of years ago at the Council of Nicaea in 325 AD. Billions of people throughout history have been imbued with the "false evidence appearing real" that allowed a handful of bishops to dictate a man-made creed that blasphemes the True God.

"Son of God" and "Sons of God" have been used throughout history. The Hebrew Bible refers to "Sons of God" several times. This means they are elected or chosen by God. It does not mean that they were equal to God. The New Testament often uses the phrase to recognize one's godly character. It does not mean they were coeternal and equal to the Father in essence and substance. Julius Caesar was deified after his assassination by the Romans. His son Augustus was called Divi filius, the Latin phrase for "son of God." Many Egyptian pharaohs were identified as a son of a deity. Although calling a person the son of God was common in ancient times, the title did not make them *equal* to God.

Hokus Pokus

A Practical Guide to Deconstruction

The definition of the word apotheosis means elevation to a divine status or deification. Millions of Americans visit the United States Capitol annually and gaze upward at the Rotunda. In 1865 Constantino Brumidi painted a fresco that took 11 months to complete. It is fifteen feet tall and 180 feet above the floor. The fresco is titled "The Apotheosis of Washington." The symbolism of the painting is shocking because it depicts George Washington becoming a god. "*The Apotheosis of Washington* depicts George Washington sitting among the heavens in an exalted manner, or in literary terms, ascending and becoming a god (apotheosis, Wikipedia, The Apotheosis of Washington.) Should Americans believe that George Washington is a god, equal to the God, coeternal, of one substance and essence?

147

Hokus Pokus

Jesus of Nazareth never referred to himself as the "Son of God." Although Jesus did not claim to be equal to the Father in substance and essence, the bishops at Nicaea did a hokus pokus, abracadabra and made Jesus of Nazareth coeternal and equal to the Father in substance and essence.

There are several verses in the New Testament where Jesus of Nazareth separates himself from the Father and affirms that God is singular and monotheistic.

Because nearly everyone can recite the "Lord's Prayer" from memory, it stands out as a definitive rebuttal to the doctrine of the Trinity and the dogma that Jesus of Nazareth is coeternal and equal to God the Father in substance and essence. The Lord's Prayer says, "Our Father which art in heaven, Hallowed be thy name. Thy kingdom come on earth as it is in heaven." (KJV). "Thy" is singular; it does not say "your" kingdom. This important point is further explained by Wikipedia "In addition, the translators of the King James_Version of the Bible attempted to maintain the distinction found in Biblical Hebrew, Aramaic and Kione Greek between singular and plural second-person pronouns and verb forms, so they used *thou, thee, thy,* and *thine* for singular, and *ye, you, your,* and *yours* for plural." The Bible translators chose this word to denote a singular monotheistic God. Although the King James Bible was published in 1611, it remains the overwhelming choice of contemporary Bible readers. Many theologians and biblical scholars will argue that the KJB is more accurate and trustworthy. Many other Bible translations use modern English, dramatically changing the text's original meaning. If one compares various translations, the modern Bibles do a hokus pokus and use the word "your" and the traditional translations, use "thy."

Luke 18:19 Jesus of Nazareth said, "No one is good except God alone."

Jesus of Nazareth, Paul, and the earliest Christians would take great offense with the Nicene Creed because it radically opposed the central teaching of Judaism. "Hear, O Israel: The Lord our God, the Lord is One." Dt 6:4

More importantly, the Doctrine of the Trinity falls apart when Yahweh is brought into the equation. By his fruits, you will know them.

Reinventing Paul

In 1969 a story was told that Paul McCartney died in a car accident. This rumor caught the attention of Beatles fans all over the world. Magazine articles, newspaper headlines, and radio talk shows fueled it. College campuses created a frenzy and jumped on the band wagon that Paul was dead. In 2010 a movie was released called the "The Last Testament of George Harrison."

In the movie, George Harrison discussed the death of Paul and the cover-up that was invented to keep the Beatles on top of the music charts. The story suggested that Paul died in a car accident on January 7, 1966, and he was secretly replaced by a look alike. William Shears Campbell was discovered in a talent show and was chosen to replace Paul. Cosmetic surgery fixed his facial features, so he looked like an identical twin of the deceased Paul.

Although the Beatles were sworn to secrecy, they provided numerous clues in their song lyrics and album covers that suggested something was amiss. The three original Beatles gave William Campbell the nickname Faul to recognize that he was a Fake Paul. This fascinating story makes one question whether the rumor about Paul's death is fact or fiction. Although the Beatles' circumstantial evidence presented a lot of clues, mainstream thinking has squashed the rumor as a hoax.

This rumor about Paul McCarthy's death and cover-up is the

background of another example of spiritual deception by the Roman Church. Like the magicians, the Roman scribes and Church fathers did a hokus pokus, abracadabra, on the Gnostic Paul and recreated him into the most prominent spokesperson for their gospel. Nearly half of the New Testament is attributed to Gnostic Paul.

The authentic Gnostic Paul would be considered a heretic and an apostate according to the orthodoxy of the Christian Church established in the Nicene Creed. The real Gnostic Paul vehemently opposed the apostles and passionately taught against their heresies. Most Christians cannot see the overwhelming evidence written in the New Testament because their spiritual eyes have been blinded by centuries of indoctrination and misinformation.

Although many scholarly books and articles support this subject, the truth about Gnostic Paul cannot be told because it would destroy the foundation of the Christian Church. Imagine what you would think if your pastor preached a mind-blowing sermon using verses from the New Testament that told the truth about Gnostic Paul. Imagine how you would feel if your pastor told you everything was a lie and a deception created by man-made religion. What if he told the congregation that Gnostic Paul was not preaching about a person, Jesus of Nazareth, but about the mystical Christ of Gnosis or the Christ within. Many would immediately walk out the door in shock and disbelief without considering what the pastor said.

The Roman Church did a hokus pokus and reinvented Gnostic Paul to make him sound like a Christian. Many scholars agree that Paul was a Gnostic writing to initiates who understood the mysteries hidden in esoteric language. More importantly Gnostics sects throughout history have called Paul the "great apostle."

This is what happens when a pastor tells the truth. In 1990, Rev. Carlton Pearson was a mega church pastor in Tulsa, Oklahoma. His congregation was one of the largest in the country, with an average attendance of over 6,000. He was one of the most popular preachers of his time, declaring the fundamentalist message about sin, salvation, heaven, and hell.

Carlton Pearson experienced a spiritual awakening and discovered that the Bible was not a literal book filled with errors, mistranslations, and misunderstandings. The bottom fell out when he told his congregation that there was no hell. His congregation went from 6,000 to 300. He was demonized and ostracized by the Christian community. He and his family suffered emotionally and financially because he told the truth.

In 2018, the tragic story of Carlton Pearson was made into a movie titled "Come Sunday." Every pastor understands man-made religion's unspoken and underlying instructions to protect and perpetuate the delusion. Carlton Pearson is a visible example of the devasting consequences for any clergyman who goes against the orthodox teachings of the Church. It also speaks volumes about seeking the truth outside the predictable, biased, and scripted answers of the Roman clergy, scholars, and apologists.

Man-made religion cannot come clean and say they are teaching hokus pokus and delusional thinking. The church is like a corporation that needs customers to stay in business.

We often think that only "lay persons" have a crisis of faith and choose to deconstruct. Many pastors and clergy are also undergoing a difficult soul-searching crisis just like individuals in their congregation. Barna Research found that 38 percent of pastors want to quit compared with 29 percent in January of 2021. Although the study does not give reasons for the high rate of dissatisfaction, one can argue that many pastors are deconstructing and have serious questions about their core beliefs. One can go online or YouTube and listen to pastors talk about their "deconstruction" journey.

Scholars and theologians often debate the topic about Gnostic Paul's true beliefs. Some argue he is a Christian while others consider him a Gnostic. If one dismisses the opinions of modern-day "experts" and takes time to study the "bedrock" of early Church history, a truth-seeker will learn that Paul was a Gnostic and the Roman Church reinvented him to make him appear to be an opponent of Gnosticism.

The "bedrock" of early Christianity was polluted with a variety of beliefs. There was no consensus or orthodox beliefs until the Council of Nicaea in 325 A.D. In the first and second centuries, Christian Gnosticism emerged as one of the largest and fastest growing groups of believers. The many of the Christian Gnostics were Marcionites who followed the esoteric teachings of Gnostic Paul.

The Roman Church covered up and buried the beliefs of the earliest Christians. They forged documents to corrupt the Gospels and letters of Gnostic Paul. Their corruption and deception was endorsed by the power of the Roman Empire and the ecclesiastical "authority" of the Church. Because the Gnostics challenged the supreme power of the Roman Church, diabolical and blasphemous methods were used to wipe out the credibility of the Gnostics. The Church Fathers fabricated hokus pokus to portray the Gnostics as heretics.

Although the Roman Church successfully buried the truth of the early Christians, the Age of Aquarius is uncovering information that reveals the corruption and deception that has blinded unawakened souls for hundreds of years. The Roman Church created the "shadows" and told the world they are real.

Hokus Pokus

A Practical Guide to Deconstruction

Marcion

Marcion of Sinope was a wealthy shipowner and Christian theologian who lived in the second century. Because he challenged the orthodox views of the Roman Church, he was excommunicated around 140 A.D. and labeled a heretic. Although his name is rarely mentioned in Church history, he was one of the most important individuals who shaped the beliefs of the emerging church in the second century.

Although Marcion was labeled a heretic, one can argue that his beliefs represent the original faith of the early Christians. The Church Fathers called him a Gnostic. His "heretical" views were widely accepted throughout the Roman Empire and challenged the supremacy of the Church. Because the threat of Marcionism was so great, the Church mounted a major counterattack to diffuse the rapidly growing church. Many of Gnostic Paul's epistles were forged to suggest that he was against Gnosticism and the Church Fathers wrote a lot of hokus pokus to slander Marcion.

Marcion compiled the "First New Testament " canon that included the Gospel of Luke and ten Pauline epistles between 130 and 140 A.D. The Roman Church needed to expand this number to twenty-seven to support their literal interpretation of the cannon and their anti-Gnostic bias. Maricon's "New Testament" did not include the Old Testament. He rejected the Old Testament and the evil god of the Hebrew Scriptures. He believed there was only a True God revealed by Jesus of Nazareth and the god of the Old Testament was evil. This is called dualism and will be discussed in greater detail later in the book. There is much more to discuss about Marcion because he is extremely important in the formation of the beliefs of the second century Christians, before the Council of Nicaea. Maricon's gnostic beliefs are similar to the Cathars who were burned at the stake by the Catholic Church in the Middle Ages.

Many of the earliest Christians believed there was a True God and an evil god because both Jesus of Nazareth and Gnostic Paul taught this idea to their followers.

There is historical evidence to argue that Paul was a Gnostic teaching a gospel that contradicts the hokus pokus of the Roman Church. The Roman Church reinvented Paul transforming him from gnostic to Christian. This deception has spiritually blinded billions of people and allows unawakened souls to believe the "shadows" are real.

There is an expression that says, "It takes one to know one." A gnostic will easily recognize another gnostic.

- The Church Fathers called Marcion a gnostic who called Gnostic Paul the only true Apostle.

- The Gnostic Gospels found at Nag Hammadi refer to Paul in the *Prayer of the Apostle Paul*

- Paulicians were members of an Armenian gnostic Christian sect who lived in the 7th century. The fundamental doctrine of the Paulicians was dualism or the believe in an evil god, the Demiurge, who is the ruler of this world, and a Good God. They used Maricon's canon which included the Gospel of Luke and 10 epistles of Paul. They also rejected the Old Testament. "The Paulicians called themselves "Good Christians" or "True Believers" and referred to orthodox Christians as "Romanists". The name 'Paulician' was used by outsiders to refer to the sect and literally means "*the followers of Paul*." The identity of the Paul for whom the movement was named is disputed. It is most likely to be *Paul the Apostle*, a figure whom the Paulicians are consistently stated as according special veneration from the earliest sources up to their apparent extinction in the early modern period." (Wikipedia)

Truth-seekers need to connect the dots and read between the lines. Many of the earliest Christians were Gnostics, the Apostle Paul was Gnostic. The Roman Church called them "heretics" and killed thousands of Gnostics in the Middle Ages because they rejected the blasphemous teachings of the Roman Church. All of this will be discussed in detail later in the book.

Because the Roman Church reinvented Paul, most Christians have no clue why the ancient gnostic writers called him "the Great Apostle." Gnostic Paul was teaching his initiates the esoteric meaning behind dying and resurrecting, he was not teaching about the historical Jesus of the Roman literalists.

Hokus Pokus

Reinventing The Logos

The translators were like magicians who could make things appear and disappear. Metaphorically speaking, their pens were like magic wands. They could silently say the words hokus pokus, abracadabra and the truth and wisdom of the ancient world instantly disappeared. The deception that they created has spiritually blinded the world for centuries.

The "logos" was a principle or a concept that the ancient Greeks and philosophers used to communicate their understanding of God. Although the "logos" was extremely important to the ancient world, modern society has little knowledge about this foundational theological principle. There were several mistranslations that "watered down" the original Greek word for logos. This is like trashing the inherent wisdom and foundational principles of democracy written into the U.S. Constitution and renaming it the "word."

The English translation is grossly inadequate and fails to carry over the original thinking of the ancient Greeks. When the manuscripts were translated into Latin, the original word for logos was changed to "verbum," which means "word." Later the Latin word for "verbum" was changed into English, and "word" was permanently imprinted on the minds of Christians. This mistranslation gives a much different understanding of the "logos" and reinvents the original understanding of the ancient Greeks and writers of the gospels.

The Hellenistic Greeks' word for "logos" has a variety of meanings that include the Divine mind of God, Divine order, Divine pattern, wisdom of God, creative force, or speech. PBS.org describes logos as "a principle originating in classical Greek thought which refers to a universal divine reason, inherent in nature, yet transcending all oppositions and imperfections in the cosmos and humanity. An eternal and unchanging truth present from the time of creation, available to every individual who seeks it. A unifying and liberating revelatory force which reconciles the human with the divine." To summarize this, reviewing this and emphasizing the key points is helpful. It is a universal divine reason above everything in the cosmos and humanity. It is an eternal and unchanging truth that always existed. It is available to everyone who seeks it and serves as a unifying force that reconciles the human with the divine. It is extremely important to fully understand the meaning of the logos because only with this knowledge can you appreciate what the Roman Church took away from you.

The Lexham Bible Dictionary defines logos as "a concept word in the Bible symbolic of the nature and function of Jesus Christ." This shallow definition reflects the superficial understanding of logos by Christian educators.

Although Plato never used the word "logos," he believed in a rational order to the universe and a oneness connecting all physical beings. Replacing the true meaning of the "logos" with a historical person would be blasphemous to the people of the ancient world who understood the esoteric meaning behind the logos.

Changing the ancient meaning of "logos" to "word" and teaching the masses that the "word" is Jesus of Nazareth, who is equal to God, is a diabolical deception. Because the translators did a hokus pokus, abracadabra, they erased the original Greek meaning for "logos" and replaced it with "word." The Church Fathers dogmatically taught that the "word" refers to Jesus of Nazareth, Son of God, equal to God the Father, coeternal, of one substance and essence.

This is not suggesting that Jesus of Nazareth did not have the Logos or the Divine Mind within him. Ancient Gnostics believed he was the "logos" sent as a "revealer" by the True God to save humanity from their ignorance. Jesus of Nazareth achieved Christ's Consciousness while he lived on earth and was sent to reveal the good news about the "Kingdom of Heaven."

Christians throughout the world are familiar with the prologue of John's gospel. "In the beginning was the word… and the word was made flesh." This is a powerful and beautiful introduction to a gnostic text. The author of John was not writing about literal things or a historical person. He used symbolism, allegories, and metaphors to communicate with the initiates who understood his writing. Anyone on the outside who lacked this secret knowledge would read the text literally and incorrectly believe that Jesus is the "word" made flesh.

One needs to read John 1 using the original meaning of logos and hear it from a non-literal understanding of the text to appreciate what the gnostic writer is saying.

Reinventing The Apostles

The feud between Gnostic Paul and the apostles was intense. They were bitter enemies because the apostles and Jerusalem church perceived Gnostic Paul as a troublemaker, false teacher, and an apostate. On the other side, Gnostic Paul called the Jerusalem Church and the original apostles false apostles, deceitful workers, and ministers of Satan. Gnostic Paul wrote in 2 Cor:13-14 "For such are false apostles, deceitful workers, transforming themselves into apostles of Christ. And no wonder! For Satan himself transforms himself into an angel of light."

It is important to see that the Gnostic Paul and the Jerusalem Church did not agree or preach the same gospel. Although this division is clear when one mindfully reads the New Testament, the truth about the two opposing gospels has been covered up for centuries. Because Gnostic Paul's esoterical gospel was labeled "heresy" and trashed by the Roman Church, the gospel of Jesus of Nazareth survived and grew into a global religion.

Hokus Pokus
A Practical Guide to Deconstruction

The Roman Church did a hokus pokus, abracadabra and reinvented Gnostic Paul, portraying him as a staunch opponent of the Gnostics. The Roman Church fabricated a lie that changed Gnostic Paul into a Christian icon. They also created a false image that Peter and Gnostic Paul were united in friendship. Christians worldwide believe Peter and Gnostic Paul shared the same faith preaching Jesus of Nazareth. They also portray Peter and Gnostic Paul as pillars of the Church. Together they are celebrated on a feast day on June 29th. This "holy day" should be recognized as the Holy Hoax Day of Peter and Gnostic Paul.

Despite the overwhelming evidence written in black and white throughout the pages of the New Testament, this perversion of the truth has been buried and covered up for two thousand years. This deception was created by falsifying Gnostic Paul's letters and inserting forgeries of Pauline epistles into the New Testament. It is estimated that between eight and eleven books of the New Testament canon were written as forgeries.

The following is a list of verses from the New Testament supporting the suggestion that Gnostic Paul and members of the Jerusalem Church were bitter enemies, and they were preaching radically different gospels. Both sides were guilty of calling out their opponent for deception and lies. Gnostic Paul was writing on two levels. He was writing to the spiritually immature, giving them the milk of literalism; he was also writing to his spiritually mature initiates, giving them the solid food of "gnosis" hidden in allegories and mystical symbolisms.

One must be careful to fully understand Gnostic Paul. For example, when he used the words, Jesus, or Jesus Christ, he was not referring to the person Jesus of Nazareth, but the mystical Christ. When he spoke of "resurrection," he had two meanings. To the literalist, it meant a bodily resurrection after one has died. To the gnostic, it meant a spiritual resurrection while one is alive through gnosis. Although it looks like Gnostic Paul was writing about a literal resurrection, this is not true. Looks can be deceiving.

Man-made religion has reinvented Gnostic Paul by changing him from a Gnostic into a Christian. When an individual mindfully reads the letters of Gnostic Paul from this understanding, one will see that Paul was writing to initiates the sacred mysteries. The gospel that Gnostic Paul was preaching was opposed to the false gospel taught by the apostles. He was preaching the Gospel of the Kingdom or the Christ within.

Mindfully read the following verses from the perspective that Gnostic Paul was preaching to initiates about the Sacred Mysteries.

Gnostic Paul

- Gal 1:8-9: But though we, or an angel from heaven, preach any other gospel unto you than that which we have preached unto you, let him be accursed. As we said before, so say I now again, if any man preaches any other gospel unto you than that ye have received, let him be accursed.

- Gal 2:4-5: And that because of false brethren unawares brought in, who came in privily to spy out our liberty which we have in Christ Jesus, that they might bring us into bondage. To whom we gave place by subjection, no, not for an hour; that the truth of the gospel might continue with you.

- Gal 2:11: But when Peter was come to Antioch, I withstood him to the face, because he was to be blamed.

- Gal 3:1-3: O foolish Galatians, who hath bewitched you, that ye should not obey the truth, before whose eyes Jesus Christ hath been evidently set forth, crucified among you? This only would I learn of you, Received ye the Spirit by the works of the law, or by the hearing of faith? Are ye so foolish? having begun in the Spirit, are ye now made perfect by the flesh?

- Rom 1:25: They exchanged the truth about God for a lie and worshiped and served created things rather than the Creator—who is forever praised. Amen.

- 1 Cor 9:4 For if he that cometh preacheth another Jesus, whom we have not preached, or if ye receive another spirit, which ye have not received, or another gospel, which ye have not accepted, ye might well bear with him.

- 2 Cor11:13-15: For such are false apostles, deceitful workers, transforming themselves into the apostles of Christ. And no marvel; for Satan himself is transformed into an angel of light. Therefore, it is no great thing if his ministers also be transformed as the ministers of righteousness, whose end shall be according to their works.

- 1 John 2:26: These things I have written to you concerning those who try to deceive you. But the anointing which you have received from Him abides in you, and you do not need that anyone teach you; but as the same anointing teaches you concerning all things, and is true, and is not a lie, and just as it has taught you, you will abide in Him.

- 2 Thes 10-12: and with all unrighteous deception among those who perish, because they did not receive the love of the truth, that they might be saved. And for this reason, God will send them strong delusion that they should believe the lie, that they all may be condemned who did not believe the truth but had pleasure in unrighteousness.

Peter

- 2 Peter 1:16: For we have not followed cunningly devised fables, when we made known unto you the power and coming of our Lord Jesus Christ but were eyewitnesses of his majesty.

- 2 Peter 2:1: But there were false prophets also among the people, even as there shall be false teachers among you, who privily shall bring in damnable heresies, even denying the Lord that bought them and bring upon themselves swift destruction.

- 2 Peter 2:2: And many shall follow their pernicious ways; by reason of whom the way of truth shall be evil spoken of.

- 2 Peter 2 17-19: These are wells without water, clouds that are carried with a tempest; to whom the mist of darkness is reserved for ever. For when they speak great swelling words of vanity, they allure through the lusts of the flesh, through much wantonness, those that were clean escaped from them who live in error.

- 2 Peter 3 15-17: And account that the longsuffering of our Lord is salvation; even as our beloved brother Paul also according to the wisdom given unto him hath written unto you; As also in all his epistles, speaking in them of these things; in which are some things hard to be understood, which they that are unlearned and unstable wrest, as they do also the other scriptures, unto their own destruction. Ye, therefore, beloved, seeing ye know these things before, beware lest ye also, being led away with the error of the wicked, fall from your own steadfastness.

- 2 John: 7-8 For many deceivers have gone out into the world who do not confess Jesus Christ *as* coming in the flesh. This is a deceiver and an antichrist. Look to yourselves, that we do not lose those things we worked for, but that we may receive a full reward.

Hokus Pokus

Gerald Massey

Paul, the Gnostic Opponent of Peter
Not An Apostle of Historic Christianity

Gerald Massey lived between 1828 and 1907. He is well known for his profound and broad expertise in many subjects, but Egyptology and Spiritualism stood out. His writings had a great influence on many truth seekers and spiritual authors. Because his knowledge overshadowed his critics, he is often misunderstood and criticized.

The following is an excerpt from Gerald Massey's Published Lectures. "My conclusion is that fabricated evidence is the sole support of Historic Christianity which can be derived from the Epistles of Paul; that the manipulation for an ulterior purpose, which is so obvious in the book of Acts, was far more subtly and fundamentally applied to his Epistles and doctrines; that they have been worked over as thieves manipulate stolen linen when they pick out the marks of ownership to escape from detection; that false doctrines have been foisted into the original text, which seems to have been withheld for a century after the writer's death until the leaven of falsehood had done its fatal work. The problem of the plotters and forgers in Rome was how to convert the mythical Christology into historic Christianity, and when Paul's Epistles were permitted to emerge from obscurity in a collection, what had occurred was the *restoration* of the carnalized Christ, that *"other Jesus"* who was repudiated by Paul in his own lifetime. Paul felt or feared and foretold that this would be the case.

When once he was removed out of the way. He saw the mystery of lawlessness already at work—the falsifiers sending forth letters as if from himself—and we have seen what Paul foresaw! The problem of the plotters who forged the foundations of the Church in Rome was how to successfully blend the Christ Jesus of the Gnostics, of the pre-Christian Apocrypha, of Philo, and of Paul, with that *Corporeal Christ* and impossible personality, in whom they ignorantly believed, through a blind literalization of mythology, so as to make the historic look like the true starting-point, and the Gnostic interpretation becomes a later heresy. This was finally affected when the declaration of John—that *"the Word was made flesh and dwelt among us"*—had been accepted as the genuine Gospel, and that which had been an impossibility for the Gnostics was an accomplished fact for those who knew no better than to believe. The Gospel, according to John, was concocted and calculated to serve as a harmonizing amalgam of doctrines that were fundamentally opposed. In this Amalgam they tried to mix the "gall and honey" so that, if "well shaken before taken," it might be swallowed by the followers on both sides. But there was a great gulf forever fixed between the Gnostic Christology and Historic

Christianity. It was a gulf that never could be soundly bridged and never has been plumbed, or bottomed, or filled in. The bodies of two million martyrs of free-thought, put to death as heretics in Europe alone, and all the blood that has ever been shed in Christian wars have failed to fill that gulf, which waits as ever wide-jawed for its prey. Across that gulf, the Christian Church was erected upon supports on either side. On one side stood those pillars of the Church which were seen by Paul in Jerusalem. On the other was Paul himself, the pillar that stood alone. A difference the most radical and profound divided him from the other apostles, Cephas, John, and James. From the first, they were on two sides of the chasm that could not be closed; and the *Prædicatio Petri* declares that Peter and Paul remained unreconciled till death. The great work of the first centuries was how to bridge the chasm over, or at least how to conceal it from the eyes of the world in later times. This could only be done by resting on Paul as a prop and buttress on the one side and Peter on the other, which had to be done by converting or perverting the Epistles of the Gnostic Paul into a support for Historic Christianity. In that way the Church was founded. It was built as a bridge across the gulf, and the Pope of Rome appointed and aptly designated *Pontifex Maximus.* It was reared above the chasm lying darkly lurking like an open grave below, and today, as ever, the Christian world is horribly haunted with the fear that a breath or two of larger intellectual life, a too audible utterance of freer thought, a dose of mental dynamite may bring the edifice of error down in wreck and ruin to fill that gulf at last, over which it was so perilously founded from the first."

Reinventing The Gospels

2 Peter 3:16 said that Gnostic Paul's writings are difficult to understand. It says that "ignorant and unstable distort them.... unto their destruction." Gnostic Paul's writings are extremely difficult and confusing if one reads them literally. This makes Gnostic Paul appear to be conflicted and schizophrenic over his teachings.

When the reader understands the basic concepts and elementary teachings of Gnosticism in the first century and second centuries, the writings of Gnostic Paul become clear and insightful. Gnostic Paul's writings are esoteric and symbolic. He used ancient mystery schools' images, words, and cryptic sayings. Gnostic Paul was a teacher of sacred mysteries and taught members of his community secret knowledge or gnosis. He used the Gnostic code words "mystery" or "mysteries" in his epistles twenty times.

Because his epistles were not written for *"those people"* on the outside, they are extremely hard to understand for anyone not familiar with Gnostic tradition. *Those people* on the outside lacked the required gnosis or sacred key of knowledge to understand the mysteries and secret teachings. The "ignorant" and "unstable" distorted Gnostic Paul's epistles and corrupted his writings with delusional ideas and hokus pokus.

Although Gnostic Paul used "Christian" words, he never used specific details about the life of Jesus. He never met the Jesus of Nazareth in person. More importantly, he did not write a single word about the virgin birth, the miracles of Jesus, his teachings, his empty tomb, nor his appearance to the women after his resurrection. Because Gnostic Paul was reaching out to Gentiles unfamiliar with the life of Jesus, it seems strange that Gnostic Paul omitted these vital details. His writings drastically differ from the contemporary apologist of the Christian faith who will offer abundant facts and overwhelming "evidence" to prove their point about Jesus of Nazareth's life. Because Gnostic Paul never wrote about the crucial details surrounding the life of Jesus of Nazareth, one needs to consider the possibility that he was not writing about Jesus of Nazareth preached by the literalists. He was writing about the mystical Christ, or Christos, known by the ancient Egyptians, Greeks, Persians, mystical thinkers, and philosophers who lived thousands of years before the birth of Jesus of Nazareth.

In Gal 1: 6-9, the Gnostic Paul scolded his students for returning to a different gospel so soon. He warned them that some pervert the gospel of Christ, i.e., the gospel of the mystical and symbolic Christ. He admonished his students with a stern warning. "As we have said before, so now I say again, if anyone preaches any other gospel to you than what you have received, let him be accursed." He later called the Galatians "foolish" and asked who deceived them.

The "other" gospel was radically different and based on the literal life of Jesus of Nazareth. This was a perversion of the sacred mysteries. Because the "ignorant" and "unstable" did not understand Gnostic Paul's writings, the "other" gospel spread throughout the land.

Gnostic Paul's words still speak the truth today…. "If anyone preaches any other gospel to you than what you have received, let him be accursed." It is important to see the two radically different gospels that opposed each other in the early church. Gnostic Paul's gospel preached the Christ of Gnosis or the Christ within, and the gospel of Peter and the apostles preached Jesus of Nazareth, a literal person.

Hokus Pokus

A Practical Guide to Deconstruction

Inspired or Uninspired

The Roman Church said hokus pokus, abracadabra and changed man-made texts into the inspired word of God, inerrant, and infallible. This deception was pushed on uneducated, gullible peasants living within the Roman Empire. These poor souls naively believed everything they were told in fear of going to hell. This mass indoctrination laid the foundation for billions of unawakened souls to collectively believe this hokus pokus hundreds of years later.

There are numerous errors, mistranslations, and contradictions that obliterate this claim. The books in the Bible are written by humans and were modified by the Roman scribes to agree with the teachings of the man-made religion. It is hokus pokus and delusional thinking when someone tells you the Bible is the "word" of God.

The Roman church hijacked the Jewish holy scriptures and comingled it with their New Testament. Can you imagine how the Jewish rabbis reacted when they learned Rome was stealing their beloved Torah and adding it to their blasphemous cannon? (By their fruits you shall know them,)

Rome used the Jewish scriptures to invent prophecies and claim they were fulfilled by Jesus of Nazareth. A closer look at the prophecies will reveal that the gospel writers did a hokus pokus to deceive the reader. The New Testament is a canon that reflects the self-serving agenda of the Roman Church.

There were hundreds of texts circulating in the ancient world that provided a different message that reflected the beliefs of the early Christians. The Gnostic Gospels were discovered in 1945 and shed a new light on the beliefs of the earliest believers. The Roman Church rejected everything that did not agree with their beliefs and called the other gospels heretical. To make sure that no one could read these heretical gospels, Rome destroyed all of them. One of the world's largest and most prominent wisdom libraries in the ancient world was located in Alexandria, Egypt. It had thousands of papyrus scrolls; estimates range from 40,000 to 400,000. This was the center of wisdom and knowledge for the ancient world.

In 391 A.D. Christians destroyed the Great Library of Alexandria, burning the all the scrolls and erasing the ancient wisdom writings. (By their fruits you shall know them) Despite Rome's effort to destroy every last scroll, a recent discovery in 1945 at Nag Hamadi brought to light hundreds of ancient Gnostic scrolls that were buried hundreds of years ago. The Dead Sea Scrolls are revealing a spiritual message that is different from the New Testament gospels and the teachings of man-made religion.

A truth seeker will soon discover all of this and much more

when the curtain of "blind faith" is removed. This book will provide disturbing evidence that man-made religion is guilty of many other atrocities. It will also explain the underlying reasons humanity allows this deception to continue.

Because most Christian scholars, historians, and apologists are biased, their perception of the truth is preconceived and often counterintuitive. Their predictable conclusions are shrouded with long fancy words and confusing sentences that a lay person does not understand. Because they have all been trained, educated, and indoctrinated in literal thinking, they do not understand the esoteric truths hidden from them.

The translators of the gospels had the monumental responsibility of providing an accurate and truthful interpretation of the Greek text. There is overwhelming evidence that the translators corrupted the sacred texts with their Roman theology and literalism. This perversion of the truth was further embellished by the Church fathers who lacked the spiritual understanding to recognize the esoteric or hidden meanings written into the gospel manuscripts.

Because the hokus pokus and delusional thinking are counterfeit spirits perpetuated by the Father of Lies, the collective unconsciousness of humanity is shackled to the wall in the cave and unable to escape. This will be explained in greater detail later in the book when the curtain is finally pulled back, and you see the real "Wizard."

This is a spoiler alert, the creature behind the curtain is a wolf in sheep's clothing. The trickster "Wizard" who is deceiving humanity is the Father of Lies, Satan, the devil, or the god of this world. He is using man-made religion to perpetuate his lies and hokus pokus to prevent unawakened souls from escaping the cave and discover the True God, Abba Father.

Size of Text Matters

The ancient Greek manuscripts were written in "all" capital letters, with no spaces or punctuation. For hundreds of years, this was the standard format that translators had to decode. Lowercase letters were estimated to be introduced between the ninth and tenth centuries. This is an important point to consider.

Did the translators of the Greek manuscripts say hokus pokus, abracadabra on the original text and intentionally deify Jesus of Nazareth into the "Son of God" equal to the Father, coeternal, with one substance and essence? Changing one letter from a lower case "l" to a capital "L" makes a monumental difference when you read the words "lord" or "Lord?" Every time a Bible reader reads a Bible passage about Jesus of Nazareth that uses a capital letter, a silent voice deceives the mind into believing the false evidence appears real. This is another example of the counterfeit spirit deceiving individuals.

"But to us there is but one God, the Father, of whom are all things, and we in him; and one Lord Jesus Christ, by whom are all things, and we by him." 1 Cor 8:6

This verse has two important points to consider. First, "it says there is but one God, the Father." This ties into the previous discussion that refutes the dogmas and doctrines of the Nicene Creed about the Trinity and proclaims the Son of God is equal to the Father.

Secondly, the text reads one Lord Jesus Christ. Because the "L" is capitalized in Lord, the translator did a hokus pokus, abracadabra and transformed Jesus of Nazareth into a divine being. Consider the possibility that the original Greek text was mistranslated, and the author intended it to read one lord Jesus Christ. (By your fruits you shall know them.) This hokus pokus has been perpetuated for two thousand years, keeping individuals trapped in a cave of delusional thinking and separated from the True God.

Properly understood, this would make Jesus of Nazareth a created being who achieved Christ's Consciousness and became one with the Father. It would make him a "son of God" but not equal to God, coeternal, or of one substance or essence.

Gnostic Paul asked his followers in Rome, "Who changed the truth of God into a lie and worshipped and served the creature more than the Creator, who is blessed forever? Amen." Romans 1:25 This verse should take on a new meaning when one wakes up and sees that the Christian church is worshipping the "creature" or created being, not the Creator. Although Paul asked this question hundreds of years ago, it still is relevant today. Billions of unawakened souls worship the "created being" and not the Creator. (This is the counterfeit spirit that Father of Lies uses to deceive humanity.) The truth of God was changed into a lie at the Council of Nicaea in 325 AD and has been perpetuated as false evidence appearing real in the modern world.

The Gospel of the Kingdom

Jesus of Nazareth was sent by the True God as a messenger to humanity to share the Good News or the Gospel of the Kingdom. It has been replaced and covered up by a false gospel. The true teachings of Jesus of Nazareth have been twisted, mistranslated, and blasphemed by the Roman Church to perpetuate a false man-made religious system.

Although the majority of the parables spoken by Jesus of Nazareth are about the Kingdom of Heaven, man-made religion rarely talks about them.

Man-made religion does not teach the Gospel of the Kingdom.

- Neither shall they say, Lo here! or, lo there! for, behold, the kingdom of God is within you. Luke 17:21

- You are the light of the world. A town built on a hill cannot be hidden. Neither do people light a lamp and put it under a bowl. Instead they put it on its stand, and it gives light to everyone in the house. Matt 5:14

(The scribes took the liberty to change lord to Lord. What if you capitalized the lower-case l and changed light to Light?)

- The Jews answered him, saying, For a good work we stone thee not; but for blasphemy; and because that thou, being a man, makest thyself God. Jesus answered them, Is it not written in your law, I said, Ye are gods? John 10:33-34

MORPHEUS

You take the **blue pill**, and the story ends. **You wake up in your bed, <u>and you believe whatever you want to believe</u>**.

You take the **red pill**, and you stay in Wonderland, **and I show you how deep the rabbit-hole goes.**

Is Flesh Singular or Plural?

"And the word became flesh" is a major obstacle for anyone unwilling to understand that John did not write this literally. The author of John was <u>not</u> referring to "flesh" as one historical person.

This is the false evidence appearing real or the counterfeit spirit that has deceived humanity for two thousand years.

What is the plural for flesh? The plural for flesh is flesh. The word "flesh" is an irregular noun that ends in *sh*. This means the word can be either singular or plural. What is the plural for fish? "Normally, the plural of "fish" is the same as the singular: "fish." It's one of a group of irregular plural nouns in English that are identical to the corresponding singular nouns (e.g., "moose," "sheep"). For example, you might write "The fish scatter as the shark approaches." (Scribbr)

The definition of flesh in the Merriam Webster Dictionary is.

4 a: human beings: HUMANKIND 
b: living beings

The Gnostics believed the "spark of the Divine" was trapped inside the bodies of human beings. "In Gnosticism, the divine spark is the portion of God that resides within each human being. The purpose of life is to enable the Divine Spark to be released from its captivity in matter and reestablish its connection with, or simply return to, God, who is perceived as being the source of the Divine Light." (Wikipedia)

One can argue that "flesh" is plural, and the author of John was writing from a Gnostic perspective. The Roman Church did a hokus pokus, abracadabra and changed the plural (human beings) into a singular person. It should be interpreted as The Word (Logos) incarnates into every human being.

Deconstruction of the word "flesh" reveals a drastically different understanding of the word *flesh* as taught by modern day theologians blinded by delusional thinking. Man-made religion and the counterfeit spirit have indoctrinated and brainwashed unawakened souls into believing *flesh* is singular. Gnostics and others understood that the word *flesh* is plural. When the Logos is made *flesh* the spark of the Divine logos indwells the souls of humanity.

Why is this important? "When you come to know yourselves, then you will become known, and you will realize that it is *you* who are the sons of the living father. (Gospel of Thomas) The ancient Gnostics and their initiates in first century Christianity understood that John used the word "flesh" to represent all of humanity. The logos or "Christ Consciousness" becomes "flesh" in everyone.

Ancient Gnostics also understood that John 3:16 was not about a historical person. Once again, the gnostic author of John was writing to initiates who understood the gospel's symbolic language and hidden message. "For God so loved the world that he gave his one and only Son, that whoever believes in *him* shall not perish but have eternal life." The "one and only Son" is the logos, divine mind, or spark of the Divine that dwells in every person. To say it another way… whoever believes in *"him"* shall not perish tells us that we must believe in the Mystical Christ <u>within</u> a person… and not someone on the outside. Jesus said the "kingdom of God" is within you" and Paul spoke of the "Christ within."

By their Fruits, You Will Know Them

A "watershed moment" is a turning point. It is the historical moment that changes the direction of history. In hindsight, it is a monumental or defining point that changes things and will never be the same. In the discussion about the false evidence appearing real, the watershed moment goes back to Emperor Constantine and the Council of Nicaea.

Today there are more than 45,000 Christian denominations in the world. Although much smaller, early Christianity was fragmented with many "denominations" or beliefs. Three Christian groups stood out: the Gnostics, the Aryans, and the literalists.

The largest group was Christian Gnostics, who based their beliefs on knowledge, and secret wisdom teachings passed down to initiates. This was called gnosis or knowing. Jesus and Paul would fit into this group because they used allegories, parables, and symbolism to teach their disciples or initiate the hidden mysteries about the kingdom of heaven. Jesus said, "Because it has been given to you to know the mysteries of the kingdom of heaven, but to them, it has not been given." Paul said, "Brothers, I could not address you as spiritual, but worldly—as infants in Christ. I fed you with milk and not with solid food; for until now you were not able to receive it, and even now you are still not able." The secret teachings of the Gnostics were meant for a selected few who were spiritually mature and ready to know the "mysteries." Because their sacred knowledge or "solid food" was never intended for the masses, only the "milk" or literal understanding was given to the "infants in Christ." The Gnostics were labeled "heretics" by the literal church and eventually disappeared.

The second group of Christians were Arians, who believed that Jesus of Nazareth and the Father were unequal. This believe was promoted by a priest named Arius, who lived in Alexandria, Egypt. Arianism maintains that Jesus of Nazareth was a creation of God who was not coeternal with God the Father. He had a different substance or essence because he was created.

Although the teaching of Arius maintained the divinity of Jesus, it opposed the Trinity and affirmed the Godhead as immutable, self-existent, and one in nature. They believed that the Father was greater than the Son. Because Arianism was growing in popularity, it became a major obstacle to the unification of the Roman Church and one of the major topics discussed at the Council of Nicaea in 325 AD.

By their Fruits, You Will Know Them

The smaller third group of Christians were the literalists who promoted their belief that Jesus of Nazareth was equal to the Father, sharing the same essence and substance, and He was coeternal with the Father from the beginning. They believed in the literal existence of Jesus of Nazareth and his physical death on the cross and bodily resurrection.

Constantine

One of the greatest sinister attempts to create a global delusion and deceive humanity was created by the Roman Emperor Constantine and the bishops at Nicaea. Because he desperately wanted to unify his empire, it was necessary to eradicate religious diversity and establish one universal religion throughout his empire. His political agenda superseded his theology. He was unconcerned about Christian dogmas, doctrines, and theological questions. He wanted the Christian bishops to reach a unanimous agreement that would legitimize the dogmas and doctrines of the Holy Roman Church. After the bishops reached an agreement, he used his supreme powers to enforce their creed and unite his empire under one religion. His self-serving political agenda of growing and unifying his empire motivated him. All the wisdom teachings of the ancient world and wise Greek philosophers were tossed aside to promote Constantine's hidden agenda of creating a unified Roman empire with one universal religion.

Constantine was emperor of Rome between 306 A.D to 337 A.D. In 312, A. D. Constantine "claimed" that he saw a fiery cross in the heavens with the words "By this sign thou shalt conquer." That night he dreamed that Christ appeared to him in robes of dazzling white, bearing a cross in his hands. He promised Constantine victory over his enemies if he would place the Chi Ro emblem on his soldiers' shields. This symbol was formed from the first two letters X and P of the Greek word for Christ. There are coins dated between 246-222 BC that were marked with the Chi Ro symbol. Although the church embellishes this story and uses it to memorialize the Constantine and his contributions to Christianity, there is absolutely no evidence to support the story. The "historian" who wrote about Constantine's vision was a biased Christian and admirer of the emperor. Although this legend is part of Church history, there is no factual or credible evidence to support the claim. Although the Chi Ro is a sacred symbol that predates Constantine by hundreds of years, the Church maintains that the Chi Ro symbol painted on the shields of the soldiers fighting for Constantine is a Christian symbol that refers to Christ.

A Practical Guide to Deconstruction

Although historians report that he waited until his deathbed before he was baptized, the church perpetuated self-serving misrepresentations by suggesting that Constantine converted from paganism to Christianity. Both historians and scholars have questioned the sincerity and credibility of Constantine's conversion. Circumstantial evidence gives clues that Constantine was still a pagan throughout his life and showed no signs of an

inward conversion. Between 313 A.D 326 A.D. coins were produced that reflect Constantine's connection to the pagan deity Sol Invictus. A small amount of these coins has survived, proving that Constantine was still a pagan long after his "conversion." These coins have his image on one side and a picture of Sol Invictus on the reverse side.

Between the Colosseum and the Palatine Hill in the center of Rome, the Arch of Constantine still stands as a memorial to the emperor who created a sinister alliance between the state and church. The arch was built in 315 A.D, three years after Constantine's victory on the Milvian Bridge and three years after his "conversion." It is 69 ft high, 85 ft wide and 24 ft deep and decorated with many telltale clues about Constantine that do not match the legend about his vision of the cross, his dream of Jesus, and his conversion to Christianity.

The ornate walls of the arch tell the truth and silently shout to the world, "You have it all wrong about Constantine." If his story was true, the symbol of the Chi Ro that he saw in the sky and the emblem that his soldiers put on their shields should have a prominent place on the structure that immortalized his legacy. Although the cross was the visible image of his conversion and the military victory on the Milvian Bridge, there was no cross on the arch. There was absolutely nothing on the arch to connect Constantine to Christianity. The arch had numerous images, statues, and reliefs of pagan deities such as Mithra and Apollo. There were life-size statues of four men wearing the skull cap of a Mithra priest at the top of the arch. The omission of Christian symbols on the arch and the abundance of pagan images bears witness to the obvious conclusion that Constantine was not a Christian and that the Church lied about his conversion.

Constantine is a saint in the Eastern Orthodox religion. His feast day is celebrated on May 21st. Although the Catholic Church did not canonize Constantine, he is still revered and esteemed for his contributions to the early church. This perversion of the truth is one of many examples that perpetuate the delusion or the false evidence appearing real. (F.E.A.R.)

Unlike the Christian version, a serious study of Constantine reveals a monster, hypocrite, egomaniac, and power monger who schemed and manipulated anything and everything that opposed his self-serving agenda. For example, historians have written that Constantine poisoned his son Crispus and then boiled his wife Fausta in a bath. "He killed Crispus when he incurred suspicion of having sexual relations with his stepmother Fausta. Constantine tried to remedy the evil: having ordered baths to be heated above the normal level, he deposited Fausta in them and brought her out when she was dead." (This adultery is attested to by the ancient historian Zosimus, Wikipedia)

Constantine hated the Jews and called them "Christ Killers."

His extreme antisemitism attacked the Jews and pushed the Roman Church away from its Jewish roots. He was influential in removing the Jewish Sabbath and Passover from the Christian liturgy. The Sabbath was changed to the Roman pagan day of worship on Sunday, and Passover was switched to Easter, another Roman pagan holiday celebrating the goddess Ishtar. Constantine even planned his funeral to leave a legacy that he was equal to the apostles. Before his death, he requested twelve cenotaphs or empty caskets that symbolized the twelve apostles. His golden casket was elevated and placed in the center. This was Constantine's final epithet to define his legacy to the Christian world.

Constantine held the title of pontifex maximus. This was the Roman religion's highest position, empowering him to legislate reforms and enforce his will. In ancient Roman history, there were many deities and cults in the pagan world, so the role of pontifex maximus was far-reaching. During the reign of Constantine, Mithra was a prominent deity associated with the cult of Sol Invictus. Religion in the ancient world was extremely complicated with all the pagan deities, various beliefs, and philosophical ideas. Constantine saw this religious fragmentation as a major obstacle to unifying his empire.

Besides all the pagan religions, two "Christianities" coexisted in the ancient world. The larger group was Gnostic

Christians who believed in the esoteric or mystical Jesus. They had a larger presence throughout the world. Gnostics believed that Jesus represented the mystical Christ or "Christ within," the soul was awakened through gnosis or knowledge. They shared their beliefs with initiates through secret esoteric teachings that the outside world would not understand. This body of believers were called Chrestians or gnostic Chrestians. (This is not a misspelling.)

There was also a smaller cult of Christians who believed Jesus of Nazareth was a real living person crucified and resurrected. Historians estimate that the number of Christians during the reign of Constantine was between 5% and 10% of the population.

Constantine's appetite for power permitted him to scheme a plan that would change the world forever. This small cult of literal Christians flourished because the power of the Roman Empire favored it and enabled the Church to convert the uneducated population through force, fear, and unlimited financial backing.

The Roman Empire subsidized huge cathedrals, basilicas, and churches. They converted pagan temples and statues of deities to portray Christian saints. Every year thousands of worshipping Catholics kiss the toe of St Peter without knowing the historicity of the figure. This statute is the pagan deity Jupiter that was removed from the Pantheon and renamed St. Peter. Beginning with his "conversion," he adopted the literal Christianity as the religion that would help unite his growing empire and establish it as the universal and unchallenged religion of his empire. Constantine seized the opportunity to exploit this small religious cult and grow it into the Empire's official religion.

Roman Orthodoxy

Just 13 years after his conversion, Constantine summoned a council of bishops to convene at Nicaea. A small group of bishops between 250 and 318 met in 325 A.D. to create a set of official doctrines and dogmas for the emerging church. The Eastern Orthodox Church affirms that 318 is the actual number of participants. The suggestion that 318 bishops attended the gathering is quite suspicious after one reads Genesis 14:14. It tells us that Abraham had 318 trained servants.

A small group of "bishops" established dogmas and doctrines that still holds believers captive today. Although Catholics and Protestants rely on the Nicaean Creed as their foundational faith and belief in the Divinity of Jesus, there is no discussion about the small group of bishops who made this monumental decision. Although there is little historical information to determine their spiritual knowledge and qualifications, billions of people worldwide have accepted their decision as a set of principles and dogmas laid down by ecclesiastical authority to establish infallible truth.

Jesus of Nazareth rebuked Nicodemus for being a master of Israel and not understanding what he was teaching. What if the bishops at Nicaea were like Nicodemus and did not understand the gospels' hidden meanings, allegories, and meanings? What if this small group of bishops were submitting to Constantine? What if this small group of bishops made the wrong decision?

Constantine, acting as the pontifex maximus flaunted his power at the council demonstrating his authority and unspoken dictatorial control over the bishops. As a bishop and biased historian, Eusebius describes Constantine at the opening ceremony of the council, "himself proceeded through the midst of the assembly, like some heavenly messenger of God, clothed in raiment which glittered as it were with rays of light, reflecting the glowing radiance of a purple robe, and adorned with the brilliant splendor of gold and precious stones." (Wikipedia) There was the threat of exile for any bishop who did not agree with the final decision of the Council of bishops. Historians have reported that three bishops did not sign the creed and they were all exiled. Constantine added an edict directed to anyone who agreed with the "heretic" Arius or even possessed some of his "ungodly" writings would be subject to capital punishment. They were later "forgiven" for their error and invited back for reconciliation.

Council of Nicaea 325 A.D.

Raise your hand if you want to make Jesus of Nazareth... Son of God, Equal to the Father, Coeternal, of One Substance and One Essence... Furthermore, anyone who does not vote "yes" will be exiled and excommunicated from the Catholic Church.

One of the heretical bishops who was excommunicated was chosen to baptize Constantine before his death. Because he was never baptized until he was on his deathbed, one can speculate that he was still a practicing pagan and deeply rooted in the paganism of Mithraism and Sol Invictus at the time of the Council of Nicaea in 325 A.D. It is important to recognize that Pope Sylvester did not summon the Council or attend the synod despite the monumental importance of the early Church's issues. The synod of bishops at Nicaea recognized the "literalists" as the infallible voice of the Christian religion and labeled all non-believers as heretics.

The Council of Nicaea established a set of dogmas and doctrines that Constantine adopted to establish a universal religion for his empire. It was far easier for Constantine to recreate a small, obscure cult and grow it than deal with a large, established pagan religion. The diabolical mind of Constantine allowed him to merge pagan beliefs and practices with Catholicism. He followed the example of the pagan sun gods and made Sunday the day of worship and replaced Passover with the pagan celebration Easter, named after the pagan goddess Ishtar.

The Nicene Creed was the official document that crucified the mystical Christ of the sacred mystery schools. The mysteries were blasphemed by a "creed" written by a small group of unenlightened bishops. This small synod of bishops pushed aside and ignored the ancient esoteric wisdom of Egypt, Greece, Rome, and philosophers like Plato who predated the Council of Nicaea by thousands of years. Although there was no scripture to support the Nicene Creed, Constantine embraced the unified Catholic Church and used it to his political advantage. He oversaw the "marriage" between religion and a secular state.

Because the Council of Nicaea established modern Christian

orthodoxy, every believer is indirectly linked to Constantine and his controlled bishops. Catholic and Protestant ministers have never shared the truth about the Council of Nicaea. They have covered the truth and allowed the Nicaean heresy to perpetuate idolatry that blasphemes the True God.

Constantine was a pagan/Christian who bought the loyalty of the bishops through bribery and passing out lavish imperial benefits. This is like modern-day lobbyists who buy votes in the US Senate and House of Congress. As a last resort, Constantine used his ruthless power to instill fear in the bishops. He threatened excommunication and capital punishment for anyone who did not follow his instructions. Constantine gave birth to "caesaropapism," a political system where the head of state is also the head of the church and supreme judge in religious matters.

It was the pagan/Christian Constantine and his controlled bishops who decided that Jesus of Nazareth was equal to God Almighty, coeternal, and having the same substance and essence. At a minimum, this is something to think about, or one can do a fact check that requires research, study, and critical thinking.

The (Original) Nicene Creed of 325 AD

We believe in one God, the Father almighty, the Maker of heaven and earth, and all visible and invisible things. And in one Lord Jesus Christ, the Son of God, the only begotten, begotten of the Father before all ages. Light of Light, true God of true God, begotten not made, of one essence with the Father by whom all things were made, who for us men and for our salvation, came down from heaven, and was incarnate of the Holy Spirit and the Virgin Mary and became man. And He was crucified for us under Pontius Pilate, and suffered, and was buried. And the third day He rose again, according to the Scriptures; and ascended into heaven, and sits at the right hand of the Father; and He shall come again with glory to judge the living and the dead; whose Kingdom shall have no end. And in the Holy Spirit.

But as for those who say, there was when He was not, and, before being born He was not, and that He came into existence out of nothing, or who assert that the Son of God is from a different hypostasis or substance, or is created, or is subject to alteration or change – *these the Catholic Church anathemizes.*

The bishops added a curse or anathema to anyone who disagreed with their statement of faith. It showed their arrogance, exclusivity, and judgmental attitude. The definition of anathema is someone or something intensely disliked or loathed, one that is cursed by ecclesiastical authority accompanied by excommunication. Historians tell us that three bishops were exiled and anathematized because they did not sign the creed.

At a minimum, one must consider if these bishops made a wrong decision and incorrectly voted to make Jesus of Nazareth equal to the Father, coeternal, of one substance and essence.

Although the Nicene Creed established orthodoxy for a unified Catholic Church and the Roman Empire in 325 A.D., it shows signs of decay and losing credibility in modern times. People are leaving institutional churches, dogmas, and doctrines, searching for a more meaningful faith. They discover that blind faith has kept them in bondage through spiritual ignorance and childish thinking.

The following is an excerpt from the Christian Post Reporter dated May 18, 2022. The title of the article is:

"Nearly 40% of Gen Z adults believe Jesus wasn't sinless: Survey."

A new study suggests that nearly one in four Gen Z adults believe Jesus was a man who sinned like everyone else rather than the incarnate Son of God of Christian orthodoxy. Polling conducted for the American Bible Society (ABS) and its latest "State of the Bible 2022" report found that 38% of people ages 18-25 believe "Jesus Christ was human and committed sins, like other people. The result is roughly in line with Gen X (37%), millennials (35%) and baby boomers (35%), who also don't seem to believe in the biblical doctrine of a sinless Christ. Americans aged seventy-seven and older believed Jesus sinned at statistically lower numbers (26%) as the group proved to be the "most likely to be Bible Users (58%) of any generation." The findings were detailed in Chapter 2 of the 2022 "State of the Bible" report released this month, featuring data compiled by ABS in collaboration with NORC at the University of Chicago.

Conversion and Genocide

Throughout the centuries, F.E.A.R. has been the primary motivation to kill millions in the name of religion. There has been a trail of blood that cannot be covered up. The Crusades were religious wars that began in the eleventh century and lasted hundreds of years. Eight major crusades between 1096 and 1291 were initiated and supported by the Roman papacy. Pope Urban II called it a holy war. He told the militants that they would receive a remission for their sins because they were fighting the enemies of God. The Crusaders would mark themselves with a cross to visually display the image of their Christian faith and justify their killing and atrocities. It is estimated that over one million people died because of this religious war. Jews were slaughtered, and entire villages were wiped out in the Rhineland of Europe.

Another military undertaking that was authorized by the papacy is known as the Inquisition. European Christians banded together to fight Muslims and recapture territories that once belonged to the Christians. Thousands of people were killed. Beginning in the twelfth century, the Catholic Church authorized the eradication of heretics and nonbelievers throughout Europe. In the name of religion, torture, brutality, and execution were used to promote the agenda of the papacy. It is estimated that between

32,000 and 300,00 "heretics" died during the Spanish Inquisition. Approximately 300,000 Jews were forced to convert to Christianity or face exile from their homeland and thousands of Muslims were burned at the stake because they refused to convert to Christianity. This will be discussed in detail later in the book.

We continue to see religious intolerance playing out in modern times. Between 1935 and 1945, approximately six million Jews were exterminated in gas chambers because of antisemitism and religious intolerance. There are ongoing conflicts between Protestants and Catholics in Northern Ireland, Jews and Palestinians, Muslims and Christians, and Muslims and Jews. Man-made religion is the root cause of much bloodshed and conflict today. Extreme religious fundamentalism fuels the passions of religious zealots and divides humanity from achieving lasting peace, harmony, and global brotherhood.

Valley of the Dry Bones

The vision of the Valley of Dry Bones is a prophecy in chapter 37 of the Book of Ezekiel. The prophet sees himself standing in a valley full of dry human bones in his vision. The Lord commanded Ezekiel to prophesize over the dry bones and breathe life into them. There was a noise and shaking, and the bones connected into human figures; then, the bones were covered with tendon tissues, flesh, and skin.

"This is what the Sovereign LORD says to these bones: I will make breath enter you, and you will come to life." Ez 37:5

Although this never happened, the metaphor comes alive as the dawning of the Age of Aquarius tears down the spiritual dark ages and brings liberation to unawakened souls. The "dry bones" may have something to say to those with "ears to hear."

Although history books briefly mention the Crusades and the Inquisition, most people are unaware of the magnitude and barbarism of these religious wars. "The Inquisition was a powerful office within the Catholic Church to root out and punish heresy throughout Europe and Muslim communities. Beginning in the 12th century and continuing for hundreds of years, the Inquisition terrorized the world during the Middle Ages. It is remembered for the severity of its tortures and its persecution of Jews and Muslims. Its worst manifestation was in Spain, where the Spanish Inquisition was a dominant force for more than two hundred years, resulting in 32,000 executions." (History.com Nov 17, 2017, and updated March 27, 2023)

Scattered throughout Europe are the "dry bones" of thousands of Christian heretics who were slaughtered, tortured, and burned at the stake by the military arm of the Catholic Church. Not only were the Jews and Muslims persecuted, but there was also a religious genocide that put the Catholic Church against other Christians. A closer look at this conflict may reveal the identity of the "true Christians or followers of Christ" and the "false Christians." The dry bones will be our guide.

Hokus Pokus

A Practical Guide to Deconstruction

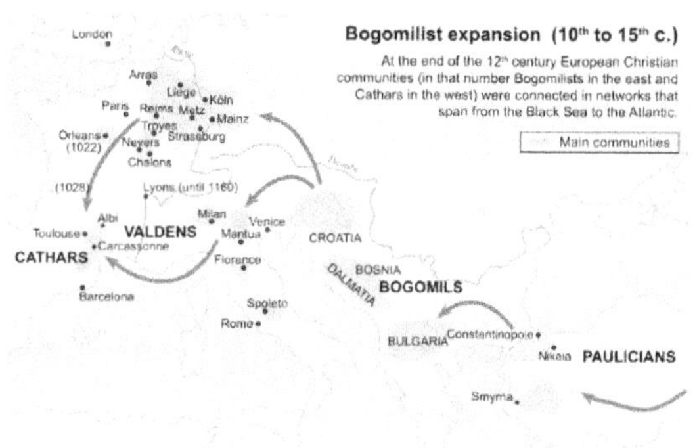

In the 12th and 13th centuries, several Christian groups broke away from the Catholic Church and flourished. In Western Europe, they were known as the Cathars. Another group called the Bogomils quickly spread over many eastern European and Asian provinces of the Byzantine Empire. Another group of "free thinkers" were the Waldensians. All of them are Europe's forgotten Gnostics. They all shared much in common and were closely related to the beliefs of ancient Gnostics. The papacy also targeted the Knights Templar. In 1310, 54 Templars were burned at the stake for their beliefs.

The presence of the heretics spread like cancer throughout Europe. Pope Innocent III called for the Albigensian Crusade to eliminate the Christian apostates. The Catholic Church did a hokus pokus, abracadabra and labeled these dissenting factions as heretics despite their religious fervor and dedication to the True God. Modern Christian apologists often add the label "heretic" as a descriptive adjective that still unjustly condemns them hundreds of years later.

215

Because these "dry bones" have been slandered and misrepresented by the Catholic Church, their beliefs, and the reason they were persecuted remain buried with their ashes. Both historians and modern-day Christians fail to condemn the Catholic Church for committing genocide and inflicting unthinkable atrocities on fellow humans.

Cathars

In the 13th century, there was a peaceful Christian community in southern France called the Cathars. They had a simple lifestyle and a profound devotion to the True God. They were known for their brotherly love, purity, and imitation of the early Christians. Thousands of Cathars were scattered throughout Western European. Languedoc, in beautiful Southern France, was the central location for the Cathars. They prayed often, fasted, and lived a holy life separate from the materialistic world. The "pure ones" believed their lifestyle represented the true Christians because their lifestyle exemplified the first-century Church and apostles. They called themselves the "church of love."

The Cathar Creed

It has no membership, save those who know they belong. It has no rivals because it is non-competitive. It has no ambition - it seeks only to serve. It knows no boundaries, for nationalisms are unloving. It is not of itself because it seeks to enrich all groups and religions.

It acknowledges all great teachers of all the ages who have shown the truth of love. Those who participate practice the truth of love in all their being. There is no walk of life or nationality that is a barrier. Those who are, know. It seeks not to teach but to be, and by being, enriched. It recognizes that the way we are may be the way of those around us because we are that way.

It recognizes the whole planet as a being of which we are a part. It recognizes that the time has come for supreme transmutation, the ultimate alchemical act of conscious change of the ego into a voluntary return to the whole. It does not proclaim itself with a loud voice but in the subtle realms of loving.

It salutes all those in the past who have blazoned the path but have paid the price. It admits no hierarchy or structure, for no one is greater than another. Its members shall know each other by their deeds and being, and by their eyes and by no other outward sign.

Each one will dedicate their life to the silent loving of their neighbor and environment, and the planet, will carry out their task, however exalted or humble. It recognizes the supremacy of the great idea, which may only be accomplished if the human race practices the supremacy of love. It has no reward to offer, either here or in the hereafter, save that of the ineffable joy of being and loving.

Each shall seek to advance the cause of understanding, doing good by stealth and teaching only by example. They shall heal their neighbor, their community, our planet and living beings in whatever form they take.

They shall know no fear and feel no shame, and their witness shall prevail over all odds. It has no secret, no arcanum, no initiation, save that of true understanding of the power of love, and that, if we want it to be so, the world will change, but only if we change. All who belong, belong; they belong to the Church of Love. (htttps://static1.squarespace.com/static/5fd7fc94c745353d202de286/t/61e9de3580080a29de317b09/1642716728115/Cathar-Creed-with-Dove.pdf)

Catholic Church and the Crusades

The insanity of man-made religion appears throughout the Middle Ages. The Catholic Church declared several crusades to wipe out the heretics; the first is known as the Albigensian Crusade, which targeted other Christians. It was a twenty-year military campaign that killed between 500,000 and one million innocent people. Crusaders were sent by the papacy to eradicate the Cathars and other heretical believers in southern France and northern Italy. On July 22, 1209, a slaughter of "heretics" took place in southern France. The inhabitants who were armed with sticks and shovels faced a garrison of approximately 3,500 heavily armed troops.

When the massacre started, the Crusaders, in the name of God, went door to door killing men, women, and children. Hundreds of residents, both Catholic and Cathars, gathered inside the Church of Mary Magdalene. Some estimates suggest that there were over 1,000 people seeking refuge inside the church. Because the soldiers could not separate Catholics from Cathars, the papal envoy gave instructions to his soldiers to "Slaughter them all and let God sort them out." The Crusaders kicked in the door and killed everyone. This atrocity is recorded as the Massacre at Beziers. The French city of Beziers was totally burned to ashes and 20,000 residents were killed in cold blood. This was an evil act of spiritual genocide committed by the vicars of Christ. By their fruits, you will know them.

The Crusaders were recruited with the promise that their sins would be forgiven if they died, so they would immediately go to heaven. There were other benefits like the forgiveness of debts, freedom from taxes, take from their conquests, and fame and fortune after they returned home. Because the Catholic Church called this a holy war, young Crusaders believed they were killing, torturing, and burning people alive in the name of God.

The atrocities of the Crusades are far worse than the evils committed by Nazi Germany in World War II. Writing about these disgusting crimes against humanity is necessary because it reveals the evil and diabolical agenda of the "Holy" Catholic Church. (By their fruits you will know them) The Crusaders used torture devices like the rack, thumb screw, and breaking wheel to inflict excruciating pain. Pope Innocent IV, in 1252, sanctioned torture as an acceptable way to obtain a confession. When a heretic refused to renounce their beliefs, they were burned alive at the stake.

The Inquisitors created a police state that the German Gestapo replicated. They would go into a city and search house to house for the heretics. They demanded everyone who came forward and made a confession to wear a yellow cross on the front and back of their garments to let everyone know they were heretics. They used scare tactics to force family, friends, and neighbors to help the Crusaders betray the Cathars. The Inquisitors used all sorts of techniques to obtain confessions and information about the whereabouts of the Cathars in hiding. They threatened to harm family members, promised leniency for confessing, and used sleep deprivation to expedite an admission of guilt. Many were placed in a dark prison with only bread and water for nourishment. If these "humane" tactics failed to break a person's will, torture devices were used to inflict excruciating pain on a person for not confessing.

The very thought that the "Holy "Catholic Church condoned spiritual genocide, inhumane torture, brutality, killing in cold blood, and burning humans at the stake is incomprehensible. By their fruits you will know them.

The Siege of Montsegur

The siege of Montsegur was a nine-month siege on a Cathar fortress where hundreds of men, women, and children gathered for safety. Approximately ten thousand Crusaders encircled the castle depriving the Cathars of food and water. The "heretics" were given a choice to surrender and renounce their faith or receive capital punishment by a raging fire. Between 210 and 215, Cathar believers did not convert and submit to the Catholic Church. They were marched down to the location where the pyre had been erected with a mountain of combustible materials. It is reported that no stakes were needed because the Cathars voluntarily walked into the fiery furnace.

"In a few hours' time the two hundred living torches heaped together inside the palisade were no more than a mass of raw, blackened, bleeding flesh, slowly burning to a cindered crisp, spreading a ghastly stench of burnt meat right down the valley, and up to very walls of the fortress" (History At Montsegur: A History of the Albigensian Crusade, Zoe Oldenbourg,) This marked the end of the last persecutions for the heretics in southern France.

Religious wars continued for hundreds of years after the Crusades. The French Wars of Religion is another example of the insanity that grips the religious mind of orthodox believers. Because religious fundamentalists are incapable of respecting the beliefs and opinions of other human beings, millions of people have been killed in the name of religion. Between 1562 and 1598, Protestants and Catholics fought a bloody war in France that killed between two and four million people.

Heretics or True Believers

These "heretics" of the Middle Ages are the precursors of the modern-day deconstructionist or deconverters. Because they chose to disassemble the religion handed down to them by the ecclesiastical authorities, they discovered the errors, delusional thinking, and hokus pokus of the Catholic Church. In modern times, truth seekers and free thinkers are using critical thinking to uncover the delusional thinking and hokus pokus from the modern-day Church system. Truth seekers are discovering that the "Wizard" is a fraud, the "Evil Witch" is out to spiritually kill them, and the "Big Bad Wolf" is a sheep in wolves clothing set out to trick and kill them.

The modern Church will not send armed soldiers to slaughter, kill, and burn individuals at the stake like in the Middle Ages. Times have changed, so their "soldiers" are the Christian apologists, theologians, and biased clergy who spiritually slaughter and kill the "seed" of truth planted in the souls of truth seekers. They weaponize their scriptures, bully, and gaslight individuals to keep unawakened souls shackled to the wall and unable to escape the cave.

Many reputable scholars will hide behind their academic degrees rooted in literalism and belittle anyone who is not equal to their "expertise." For example, Bart Ehrman, a well-known New

Testament scholar and author, says this about Timothy Freke, "He doesn't know much about ancient history Ehrman says of Freke. "He's not a scholar. All he knows is what he's read in other conspiracy books." (CNN, March 7, 2017) This absurd comment is about someone who has written thirty-five books that have been translated into fifteen languages about Gnosticism.

Jesus of Nazareth used the Parable of the Sower to warn people about the "birds" who are out to take away the truth. "As he was scattering the seed, some fell along the path, and the birds came and ate it up." Matt 13:4 The "birds" are the false teachers, Christian apologists, and biased clergy who are the "soldiers" assigned to eradicate the heretics of the modern world.

Although the Bogomilist, Cathars, Waldensians, and Gnostics believed many things outside of orthodox beliefs, their daily lives exemplified a Christlike lifestyle. This contrasted with the immoral, materialistic, corrupt, and hypocritical Catholic clergy. The Catholic Church did a hokus pokus and labeled them heretics They failed to look in the mirror to see their own vices, corruption, and errors. At the end of this chapter/book, it will be clear that the true believers were the heretics brutally killed and slaughtered by the Catholic Church. By their fruits you shall know them.

The term Bogomil means "dear to God." The Cathars called themselves "Good Christians." Their Gnostic view is not a religion, but a worldview wrapped in myth and experience rather than dogmas and creeds. It is spirit based and comes from a higher knowledge or gnosis received from the inner being of an individual; it does come from the ecclesiastical dictates of a man-made religion.

Because their beliefs have been erased by the man-made religion, the remaining information merits mindful consideration and critical thinking. Christian historians and apologists have propagandized the truth about the Cathars. They want people to view them like the "whacko" Branch Davidians who died in a fiery furnace for their beliefs. (Just like the 220 Cather martyrs who were burned alive at Montsegur in 1343)

There is a sinister reason the Church did/does not want the beliefs of the "heretics" to come out in the open. It is time for modern take truth seeks and deconverters to listen to the "dry bones" of the heretics. Many of their beliefs are thousands of years old and go back to antiquity. Because the beliefs of the heretics were radically opposed to orthodox views, they were killed, tortured, and burned at the stake to silence their religious beliefs.

"Modern-day research is illuminating the Cathars of the Middle Ages and discovering a drastically different perspective. "Contemporary research now indicates that far from being the evil monsters that Pope Innocent III (1161-1216) decreed should be exterminated, the Cathars were devout, chaste, tolerant Christian humanists who loathed the material excesses of the medieval church. Beliefs similar to theirs can be found in the Gnostic gospels, in the Essenic teachings discovered at Qumran, and in the Egyptian mystery schools." (The Free Dictionary by Farlex, Cathars)

What the Heretics Believed

The Heretics (Bogomilists, Cathars, Waldensians, and Gnostics) were against ecclesiastical authority. They viewed the Roman Church as corrupt, materialistic, and worldly. It was apparent to them that Roman Church intentionally corrupted scripture, invented new doctrines, and abandoned the beliefs and practices of the early Christians. They characterized the Catholic Church as a "Church of Wolves." The Heretics did not recognize the authority of the pope. Their meetings were held in homes or nature because they did not believe in lavish church buildings. The Heretics honored and respected the equality of both men and women; gender was not an obstacle for women to hold higher responsibility. Like the earliest Christians, they recognized no authoritative priesthood. They appointed bishops as "supervisors."

The Heretics did not believe in the Trinity, nor did they believe Jesus of Nazareth was equal to God, coeternal, of one substance and essence. He was neither God nor man, but a manifestation of the Holy Spirit sent by the "Good God" to show us how to return to our spiritual home. There is no original sin; St Augustine invented this man-made doctrine. The heretics believed that every child was/is born in the state of an immaculate conception or free from sin. They were pacifists and condemned all killing, including war and capital punishment.

Hokus Pokus
A Practical Guide to Deconstruction

The heretics did not believe in a literal hell or eternal punishment after one dies. They believed that "hell" was limited to the chaos and sufferings of the human experience during their lifetime. They believed in reincarnation and the soul's return into a new body. (The idea of reincarnation was a widely accepted belief by early Christians, Gnostics, and philosophers like Plato. The Catholic Church did a hokus pokus in 553 AD and deemed the notion of reincarnation false. This marked the end of the debate about hell and opened the door to the delusional belief of eternal damnation.

The Heretics also believed that anyone attached to the material world was a disciple of the bad god. They pointed to the Pope as the richest man in Europe and the luxurious lifestyle of the cardinals and bishops. (Does this sound familiar?) "There was no escaping the logical conclusion that Roman Catholics worshipped the wrong God - the God of Evil who had created this world. The behavior of devout Catholics seemed to confirm this conclusion. Cathars referred to the Roman Church as the Church of Wolves." (Cathar.info Implications of Cathar Beliefs)

The Heretics believe in the ultimate salvation of all human beings through knowledge or gnosis. The Heretics and ancient Gnostics believed that divine esoteric knowledge released the soul from the bondage of ignorance. The highest level of this wisdom was granted to   elite members who spent long periods in contemplation, education, and purification. Cathars, who wished to live a life of extreme "holiness and separation from the world," participated in the ritual of spiritual initiation; this was the rite of Consolamentum. Those who chose this path were called Parfaits.

They rejected the brutal concept of blood sacrifice and vicarious atonement. The idea that the Good God would send "His Son" into an evil world and allow him to undergo crucifixion was unimaginable for a Cathar. (They believed that Jesus of Nazareth could not undergo a physical crucifixion or a physical resurrection because he was a manifestation of the Holy Spirit and only appeared like an angel)

"A part of the Good God was trapped in all men and women, longing to rejoin its Maker. The Bad God filled humankind with many temptations to frustrate souls from ever making that reunion. Although the heretics could be tortured by disease, famine, and other travails, including man's inhumanity to his fellow man, the Bad God had no power over the soul - a divine spark of the Good God." (Cathar.info Cathar Beliefs)

The following is an account of how they saw themselves, recorded around 1143 or 1144 by Eberwin, Prior of the Premonstratensian Abbey of Steinfeld, writing to Bernard of

Clairvaux (St Bernard): "Of themselves, they say: "We are the poor of Christ, who have no fixed abode and flee from city to city like sheep amidst wolves, are persecuted as were the apostles and the martyrs, despite the fact that we lead a most strict and holy life, persevering day and night in fasts and abstinence, in prayers, and in labor from which we seek only the necessities of life. We undergo this because we are not of this world. But you, lovers of the world, have peace with it because you are of the world. False apostles, who pollute the word of Christ, who seek after their own interest, have led you and your fathers astray from the true path. We and our fathers, of apostolic descent, have continued in the Grace of God and shall so remain to the end of time. To distinguish between us and you, you and us, Christ said, "By their fruits, you shall know them." Our fruits consist in following the footsteps of Christ."

Scattered throughout Yugoslavia, there are approximately 30,000 tombstones that go back to the Bogomils who lived in the Middle Ages. Many of them have raised their hands. One can speculate about the meaning of this.

It may suggest that the deceased person praises the true God in the afterlife. These "dry bones" have no voice to tell the world what they believed and how badly the Catholic Church persecuted them.

Dualism

The heretics were dualists. Dualism is an ancient philosophy that is often pictured in the imagery of Yin and Yang. The principle suggests that all things exist as inseparable and contradictory opposites. Neither side is superior to the other; harmony is achieved when both sides are in balance.

This ideology or belief was rooted in antiquity and existed long before the Middle Ages. The concept of dualism centers on the notion that everything can be seen in pairs, life and death, good and evil, hot and cold, male and female, light and darkness, etc.

The Cathars and other Gnostics groups believed in two universal principles, a good God and a bad god. The Heretics saw the "god" of the Old Testament as evil, malevolent, and inferior to the Good God of the New Testament. Yahweh was an angry and jealous god who instructed the Israelites to destroy every living thing. He was a war god, a tyrant and sadistic ruler.

Now go, attack the Amalekites and totally destroy all that belongs to them. *Do not spare them; put to death men and women, children and infants, cattle and sheep, camels and donkeys.* 1 Sam 15:3

Gnostic Paul was referring to this lower god when he referred to the "god of this world" in 2 Cor 4:4. He wrote, "In whom the god of this world hath blinded the minds of them which believe not, lest the light of the glorious gospel of Christ, who is the image of God, should shine unto them."

The Gnostics called this evil god the demiurge, Yaldabaoth, Samael, and Saklas. The Cathars called the lower god Rex Mundi, or King of the World. Today modern religions use the name Satan. The Gnostics and Cathars rejected the Old Testament. They believed the Good God was the creator of the spiritual realm and the evil god was the creator of the physical world. Because the lower god created the physical world, the heretics believed the physical world was evil and still under the control of the demiurge or Rex Mundi.

Although this sounds unbelievable and extremely strange, Gnostic Paul wrote about this in his New Testament epistles. He used "gnostic" words that his followers understood. They knew he was talking about the evil forces controlling this planet. God of this world, powers, and principalities were words that Gnostic Paul used to describe the demonic forces and evil overlords who control this world.

Maya

This book has covered a lot of issues that revolve around the hokus pokus, abracadabra of man-made religion, the false evidence appearing real, the bishops at the Council of Nicaea, and the atrocities committed by the Catholic Church during the Crusades. All of this was an introduction to prepare the reader for the moment of truth. This is when the curtain is pulled back, and the "Wizard" is revealed.

Because man-made religion has blocked the teachings and wisdom of the ancient world, humanity has lived in the spiritual dark ages for two thousand years. The ideas presented in this chapter are not new. They have been around for thousands of years.

At the very beginning of this book, we briefly discussed "illusions." On page 3 of this book there was a promise to the reader, if you keep reading this book, you will learn about the ultimate mind-blowing illusion that has been mocking your brain and tricking you into seeing something that is not real. It is the greatest illusion ever created because it makes the universe disappear.

Satan, the demiurge, Rex Mundi is the god of this world. He is the father of lies, a deceiver, evil, and malevolent trickster. He is also a the greatest "magician" of all time because he did a hokus pokus, abracadabra and made the universe disappear. The world you think is real is just an illusion, a fake reality, a shadow created by the demiurge to imprison humanity.

If you are honest with yourself, we live in a hellish nightmare. The world is in a psychotic mess; billions of people have been killed in wars. There is disease, famine, and suffering everywhere. More importantly, the larger part of humanity believes they are separate from God.

We have all asked ourselves why a loving God permits suffering, famine, sickness, wars, etc. How can a loving God send souls to eternal damnation? The simple answer…. The True God has not changed. He/She is still all-loving and does not permit bad things to happen or send souls to eternal damnation. It is the lower god, the demiurge, who is ruling this planet and pouring out confusion, chaos, evil, and suffering on humanity.

The Gnostics believed the lower evil god, the demiurge, Rex Mundi, Satan, or the God of this world, created evil and continues to create chaos, suffering, and separation. These evil forces created an illusion or a fake reality to trap humans inside a simulation. It is like a lucid dream that is so real that you cannot tell the difference between the real world and the dream world… until you wake up. Like the song says, "Row, row, row your boat; life is but a dream."

Hokus Pokus

A Practical Guide to Deconstruction

The definition of the word maya means illusion.

ma·ya

noun

HINDUISM

the supernatural power wielded by gods and demons to produce illusions.

o   HINDUISM•BUDDHISM

the power by which the universe becomes manifest; the illusion or appearance of the phenomenal world.

It is important to comprehend that "maya" is a supernatural power wielded by "gods and demons" to produce illusions.

The persecuted Cathars and Gnostics also believed that the real world was the spiritual realm, and the physical world was a fake reality. Although this sounds like something from the Twilight Zone, it is supported by modern science, quantum physics, Eastern religions, and ancient philosophers. Hollywood has made "a boat load" of movies to introduce the Gnostic concept of a fake reality. Movies

239

like Dark City, the Matrix trilogy, the Truman Show, Pleasantville, 1899, and many others are labeled Gnostic. (For a complete list, search "Gnostic movies" online, and you will be amazed at all of the popular movies with Gnostic themes.) It is interesting to note that the number of Gnostics movies mushroomed at the turn of the century, or the dawning of the Age of Aquarius.

In Plato's Allegory of the Cave, the shadows are the fake reality, and the light at the cave's opening represents the Good or the true spiritual reality. The cover on the front of this book shows prisoners shackled to a wall staring at shadows on a wall. A picture is worth a thousand words.

The blockbuster movie, The Matrix, depicts fake reality as a simulation. Artificial intelligence created the Matrix to use humans as an energy source. Humanity was trapped inside a virtual reality program called the Matrix that tricked everyone into believing there was no difference between true reality and the Matrix simulation. Agent Smith is a fictional character in the Matrix movie who represents the archons or evil rulers of the fake reality who are sent to keep unawakened souls trapped in the illusion or simulation.

The simulation hypothesis is the scientific name for a fake reality. "The simulation hypothesis proposes that our existence is a simulated reality, such as a computer simulation. This simulation could contain conscious minds that may or may not know that they live inside a simulation. This is quite different from the current, technologically achievable concept of virtual reality, which is easily distinguished from the experience of actuality. Simulated reality, by contrast, would be hard or impossible to separate from "true" reality. Much debate has been over this topic, ranging from philosophical discourse to practical applications in computing." (Wikipedia)

Even Bank of America said something about the fake reality. "Analysts at Bank of America have reportedly suggested there is a 20 to 50 percent chance our world is a Matrix-style virtual reality and everything we experience is just a simulation." The report also said that if our world was an illusion, we would never know about it. (Business Insider, Jacob Furedi, the Independent September 14, 2016)

A Course in Miracles is a book first published in 1976 that has sold over two million copies. The very first page of the book makes a fundamental distinction between the real and the unreal or knowledge and perception. Everything that God has created is real. It has no opposite, no beginning, no end, and cannot be changed. The world of perception is not real because it is based on interpretation, not on facts, and it is changeable. It is a world of birth, death, scarcity, loss, and separation. The perception of this world appears to be real, but it is an illusion. When you are caught up in the world of perception, you are caught up in a dream. (Course in Miracles, page 1)

Public awareness of a fake reality or simulation is growing rapidly. The internet has a lot of content and interviews that take this idea from weird and far out to mainstream thinking. Elon Musk believes there is a 99% chance that we are living in a fake reality. When celebrities and famous people start talking about a fake reality, one can expect that there will be an influx of curious minds who want to check it out.

Virtual Reality

In 2022 roughly 37.7 million people owned a VR headset. The images created on the headset are mind-blowing because they appear to be real and life-like. It is a fake reality. One can travel to Egypt, see the Pyramids, visit the Grand Canyon, or magically travel through outer space. VR goggles create an illusion that changes computer images into an experience that tricks the mind and senses into thinking that virtual reality is real. In the next few years, virtual reality will dramatically improve, and the user experience will be even more realistic.

The definition of virtual reality is a set of images and sounds produced by a computer that represents a place or a situation that a person can take part in. (Cambridge Dictionary) Virtual Reality is a modern-day introduction to the duality of real and fake worlds.

It was noted that Hollywood is introducing Gnostic ideas and concepts in their movies. Before seeing and appreciating what Hollywood embeds in their Gnostic movies, one must do some homework. It is necessary to spend time learning about Gnosticism and what they believed. It is not a religion with dogmas and creeds. It is an ancient worldview based on knowledge or gnosis. When the Catholic Church killed off the heretics during the Crusades, they inflicted a spiritual genocide on the sacred knowledge and gnosis of the ancient world. Having a basic understanding of Gnosticism helps one see and understand the hidden symbolisms and meanings in these movies.

The Gnostics and Cathars believed an evil god created a fake reality that trapped humans inside an illusion. The illusion is so realistic that people believe it is real. Gnostics used the Coptic word HAL to describe a simulation or virtual reality. In the movie 2001 Space Odyssey, one of the main characters is HAL. This was no accident. HAL is programmed with artificial intelligence and is described as the most sophisticated computer ever built. He is the brains of the mission.

HAL changes from a likable character to a malevolent evil entity who decides to kill the astronauts. HAL is represented in the film as an All-Seeing Eye, a symbol of God. HAL is not God but a counterfeit spirit of God who is out to destroy the mission. When crew member, James Bowman, wakes up to HAL's identity, he unplugs the computer, and HAL dies.

The Space Odyssey can be viewed as a Gnostic movie with HAL representing the demiurge or lower evil god controlling the flight. He was given a secret mission and ordered by NASA to lie to the crew members. The movie gives clues that everything is a simulation or an illusion. When crew member, James Bowman, kills HAL, he is released from the simulation or fake reality. In the end, he is free and transformed into an immortal entity.

The Wizard in the movie, The Wizard of Oz, can also be viewed as a demiurge. He was the character behind the curtain, pushing buttons and blowing smoke. The Wizard was a tyrannical ruler who ruled by fear and manipulation. He was a fraud with little or no power who deceived Dorothy, telling her he would help her go home.

Why Are There So Many Gargoyles On Cathedrals?

Why are so many creepy gargoyles looking down at the streets of cities worldwide from cathedrals and churches? After reading this book, the reader should know the answer. The Catholic Church did a hokus pokus, abracadabra and insisted that the gargoyles that adorn the majestic cathedrals worldwide are decorative downspouts and they keep away evil spirits. The primary purpose of the gargoyle is to illustrate evil. During the Medieval Ages, the Church wanted to convey a terrorizing image of evil that was carved in stone depicting the horrors of eternal damnation. The Catholic Church chooses to whitewash the sinister and diabolical symbolism of the gargoyles. Calling them decorative should be laughable to a truth seeker waking up to hokus pokus.

Hokus Pokus
A Practical Guide to Deconstruction

The silent voices of the demonic and satanic gargoyles speak truth to those with ears to hear… The Roman Catholic Church adorns itself with hundreds of demonic images because it is intrinsically evil, diabolical, and controlled by the demiurge and his helpers, the archons. The persecuted Cathar heretics were correct in their belief about the Catholic Church; it has a history of bloodshed, corruption, immorality, scandals, and materialism. Is there a sinister reason that explains why hundreds of stone images of evil and demonic creatures appear on European cathedrals and churches? (By their fruits, you shall know them.)

The definition of a gargoyle is "an ugly creature or head cut from stone and attached to the roof of an old church, etc., often with an open mouth through which rainwater flows away." Although the grotesque images of gargoyles that decorate Gothic architecture are everywhere, few people look at them and try to figure out why there are so many gargoyles on churches and buildings. Why are there so many demonic-looking creatures looking down at us? To better appreciate the universality and magnitude of these demonic stone images, one must go online and search "gargoyles gothic architecture" and click "images." The search results are mind-blowing.

There are other creepy figures in architecture. When a

decorative image does not contain a waterspout, it is referred to as grotesque or chimera. The Chapel of Bethlehem in France has twenty-eight modern grotesques. They can be found worldwide and in the most unlikely places. In Des Moines, Iowa there are twenty-eight grotesques on the Polk County Courthouse. If you look at the top of an old building, a gargoyle or grotesque may be looking down at you.

Many believe these creepy gargoyles are spiritual protectors of churches, scaring off demons and evil. One can argue this point by suggesting the stone images of gargoyles roosting on cathedrals and churches are images of the invisible demonic spirits that rule over this world. There is a slang expression that uses the phrase "come home to roost." The hundreds of gargoyles "adorning" cathedrals is a visual image of the demons coming home to roost.

They represent the principalities, powers, and evil forces of darkness that Gnostic Paul wrote about.

For we wrestle not against flesh and blood, but against *principalities, against powers, against the rulers of the darkness of this world, against spiritual wickedness in high places.* Eph 6:12

One of the most famous Gothic cathedrals in the world is the Notre Dame Cathedral, where 102 creepy gargoyles, demons, and monsters watch over the streets of Paris. The National Cathedral in Washington, DC, is also adorned with gargoyles. There are two gargoyles in the Denver airport watching over the east and west baggage claim areas. Two gargoyles are perched atop the Eastern State Prison in Pennsylvania. One of the oldest colleges in Oxford, England, has several gargoyles staring down. The Chrysler Building has several gargoyles looking down at the streets of New York. There are grotesque, demon-like figures at Westminster Abby in London. They are also found in Japan, Portugal, Germany, and many other locations worldwide.

Invisible Rulers

This is a complicated subject because most people are not familiar with archons. There is a risk of providing too much information and the reader is overwhelmed and stops reading the rest of the book. On the other hand, there is also the risk of not providing enough information and the reader skims over it, missing some life-changing insights.

Ancient Gnostics, Greeks, Egyptians, and philosophers like Plato believed there are two Gods, the True God and a lower god who created the world. They viewed the god of the Old Testament as the malevolent, tyrannical, and evil demiurge. He is the false *"god of this world"* who keeps unawakend souls trapped in their physical bodies. He inflicts pain, suffering, chaos, and tribulations on humanity to keep unawakened souls ignorant of the spark of the Divine that is planted in every person. Plato wrote about the demiurge in his dialog Timaeus and Gnostic Paul wrote about the "god of this world in the New Testament.

In whom the god of this world hath blinded the minds of them which believe not, lest the light of the glorious gospel of Christ, who is the image of God, should shine unto them. 2 Cor 4:4

And you hath he quickened, who were dead in trespasses and sins; Wherein in time past ye walked according to the course of this world, according to the prince of the power of the air, the spirit that now worketh in the children of disobedience: Eph 2 1-2

The True God sent Jesus of Nazareth to reveal the truth about the demiurge and help humanity escape through gnosis or knowledge. The True God sent Jesus of Nazareth as a revealer to preach The Gospel of the Kingdom to those with "ears to hear."

Neither shall they say, Lo here! or, lo there! for, behold, the kingdom of God is within you. Luke 17:21

Jesus of Nazareth rebuked the Pharisees and told them they belonged to the devil or the demiurge. John 8:44 speaks to all man-made religions. This verse is mind blowing when one understands what it means. Jesus of Nazareth was also speaking to all "believers" living in the twentieth century who follow the fundamental beliefs written in the Nicene Creed. The Original Nicene Creed is written word for word in this book. Read the Creed again and then read John 8:44.

You belong to your father, the devil, and you want to carry out your father's desires. He was a murderer from the beginning, not holding on to the truth, for there is no truth in him. When he lies, he speaks his native language, for he is a liar and the father of lies. John 8:44

Unawakened souls unknowingly continue to worship and pray to the Demiurge. The Father of Lies has created a counterfeit spirit that deceives unawakened souls into believing a lie. The demiurge arrogantly commands his followers to have no other gods before him. Man-made religion is a creation of the demiurge to deceive humanity and prevent them from "knowing" the True God.

Archons

The Demiurge has subordinate helpers. Cultures throughout the world have different names but they fundamentally agree that they were the builders of the physical universe and sent to inflict pain, suffering, and chaos on humanity. Ancient Gnostics used the name archon. By definition, an archon is a ruler. In the proper context, they are evil rulers who not only control the world, but also influence the thoughts and actions of humans.

The actual name of this "parasite" does not matter because numerous cultures, tribes, and civilizations throughout the world have created their own names for this demonic spirit. These invisible malevolent parasites have been on earth since the dawn of civilization, ruling over the thoughts and actions of humans. They are like covert tapeworms sucking the energy and life out of individuals, families, and society, feeding on negative emotions like fear, guilt, shame, anxiety, and condemnation.

The archons spread confusion and chaos which attacks the mind, soul, and body. Archons are responsible for depression, mental disorders, addictions, suicides, and many other human abnormalities. Because the demonic spirit is like a virus, it is contagious and quickly spreads to other humans. This produces a collective unconsciousness or collective psychotic disorder that affects large groups of people, communities, and nations.

Other worldwide cultures and civilizations used different names for this demonic spirit. Fallen angels, Nephilim, Anunnaki, reptilian, UFO's, aliens, demons, devils, and wetiko are other names used to represent the same idea. Modern day conspiracy theorists use names like cabal, illuminati, and deep state when they want to talk about dark forces and rulers of this world. This does not mean they understand this subject, but they do recognize "something" is controlling the elite power brokers in our world. Muslims recognize Jinn as the unseen spirit that inhabits the earth. Jinn or Djinn is capable of assuming various forms and exercising extraordinary powers that cause physical and mental harm to humans.

Native American Indians used the word "wetiko" to portray a cannibalistic spirit that possesses human beings. The cannibalistic nature of wetiko does not mean that it eats human flesh, wetiko devours the soul of a person and feeds off the lower emotions. This is similar to the Gnostic understanding of the archons as evil rulers. Both are like malevolent parasites that infect the psychic and raise havoc with a person's thoughts, emotions, and actions. Wetiko is a modern-day version of the Gnostic archons and the principalities and powers of darkness in the New Testament.

When the first European settlers came to America, native Americans said that they were infected by wetiko. The white invaders treated the natives as inhuman savages. They stole their property, spoiled their land, and killed millions of Native Americans. Christopher Columbus was a slave trader who amassed a fortune by enslaving thousands of Indigenous people and sending them to Spain. History sheds a dull light on the atrocities of white Americans and their treatment of indigenous people. This is a perfect illustration of wetiko and the control it has over the minds of individuals and governments.

During the Covid 19 pandemic, there was a passionate desire to determine the source of the virus. Many argued it started in China. The source of the wetiko virus is most disturbing because it came out of the Vatican.

Wetiko and the Vatican

The Pope gave us legal authority to take possession of your land. You have no rights. You are enemies of Christ and subject to our authority over you.

The inhumane atrocities of *"wetiko"* have a direct link to the archons manipulating the Vatican. The Doctrine of Discovery is the term that consolidated several fifteenth century papal bulls. In 1452 Nicholas V issued a papal bull outlining the conquest of North and South America by the European explorers. The documents stated that any land or territory not possessed by Christians was available to be "discovered" and claimed by the "Christian" discoverers. It sanctioned the enslavement of the non-Christian natives in Africa and the New World.

Because the indigenous people were considered pagans, savages, and heathens, the Catholic Church justified the inhumane and immoral takeover and conquest of their property, human rights, and their spirituality. This permitted the exploitation, enslavement, and cancel culture of millions of innocent people. The Doctrine of

Discovery influenced international law for centuries and carried over into the fabric of American law and politics. It sanctioned the genocide of native Americans and inspired the Monroe Doctrine and Manifest Destiny that perpetuated the genocide of the original inhabitants of our country. This is a brief overview of the Doctrine of Discovery. It is very important if one desire to learn more about the "wolf in sheep's clothing." The Catholic Church is responsible for the "wetiko" that established a religious, political, and legal justification for the seizure of land by the European settlers. Millions of indigenous natives were killed in North and South America for the sake of religion. Although this is the largest genocide in the history of the world, it has been covered up and buried by the wolf in sheep's clothing. The shadow of this evil atrocity still hangs over the modern world.

Counterfeit Spirits

This topic is particularly important because it explains how the demiurge hijacked man-made religion. Using the highest level of trickery and deceit, the demiurge crafted a counterfeit spirit to replace the True God. In Gnostic literature, Yaldabaoth declares, "I am God and there is no other!

The definition of counterfeit is "made in the exact imitation of something valuable or important with the intention to deceive or defraud." (Oxford Languages) The only way to detect counterfeit money is to hold the bill up to the light and see if there is the security strip running from the top to bottom.

This next section will be extremely disturbing because it will reveal the "counterfeit spirit" by holding it up to the Light. *Gnosis, Divine Knowledge*, or the *Divine Light* is the only way to detect a counterfeit spirit. Because this information is mind blowing, one needs time to digest it. It is ok to just say to yourself, "Before I reject it, I will at least think about it."

One can go online and read about the counterfeit spirit from a Christian perspective, and it will sound identical to what you will read in the next few paragraphs. They will quote scripture verses from Gnostic Paul and tell their readers that Satan is a deceiver and liar. What they say is absolutely true… whatever things that God does we find the devil attempting to counterfeit. They also teach that the devil appears as an angel of light. But their interpretation of the counterfeit spirit is hokus pokus.

Because Christian pastors, theologians, and apologists are in a delusion, they believe a lie. 2 Thes 2 11-12 They are unable to separate the counterfeit spirit from the true spirit. It is important to continually remind yourself of this important guidepost… You will know them by their fruits. A bad fruit or a bad tree is not a credible source to identify a counterfeit spirit because *they are the counterfeit spirit.*

The Gnostic Gospels write about the counterfeit spirit in The Secret Gospel of John and The Pistis Sophia. Because the Catholic Church called the Gnostics heretics and destroyed the wisdom libraries and wisdom scrolls, few people know about these ancient writings. When the Dead Sea Scrolls were discovered in 1945, the ancient beliefs of the Gnostics were made public to the modern world. Unawakened souls called out by Aquarius are being led to the Gnostic Gospels for the mind's true liberation. Without a basic understanding of Gnosticism, the New Testament is easily misunderstood and distorted.

The counterfeit spirit is described in the Gnostic Gospels as a deceptive spirit that leads humanity away from spiritual enlightenment and the True God. The Gnostics believed that Jesus of Nazareth was sent by the True God as a "revealer" who would save man from ignorance and reawaken the spark of the divine within every soul. It was Divine knowledge or gnosis, not blood atonement, which saved mankind from the "sin" of ignorance. The counterfeit spirit is a diabolical deception by demonic principalities, and powers of darkness that lead humanity away from the True God. The counterfeit spirit is so believable, it has fooled people for nearly two thousand years. It is like the shadows on the wall of Plato's cave, they were so real the prisoners did not want to leave the cave because they thought the shadows were real.

The archons are invisible parasites or virus-like psycho-spiritual creatures that take possession of our minds and change the truth into a lie through the counterfeit spirit. They imprison unawakened souls and prevent them from escaping the fake reality and returning to humanity's spiritual home with the True God.

The counterfeit spirit that infiltrated man-made religion keeps people in bondage and ignorance of our true nature. They deceive unawakened souls into worshipping a false god or a "shadow" of the True God. The counterfeit image created by the archons is so realistic that it is extremely difficult to discern the wolf in sheep's clothing. Individuals who choose to leave the "cave" are more likely to recognize that the "shadows" or counterfeit spirit are not real.

"For we wrestle not against flesh and blood, but against principalities, against powers, against the rulers of the darkness of this world, against spiritual wickedness in high places." Eph 6:12

The invisible archons and wetiko parasites rule over our thoughts, emotions, and actions spreading like a contagious virus with other humans. They started wars, slavery, bigotry, corruption, racial hatred, and countless atrocities. They control every part of our human existence. The counterfeit spirit infiltrates governments, education, banking, the military industrial complex, man-made religion, etc. All of these are subordinate to the powers of darkness to keep us trapped in a fake reality or illusion.

There are several verses in the New Testament that warn people about counterfeit spirits. Christian pastors, teachers, and apologists have no clue that Gnostic Paul was warning his followers about the Gnostic understanding of the counterfeit spirit that leads people away from the True God. Christianity is the counterfeit spirit because it leads people away from the True God and substitutes a false god for individuals to worship. This deception is the magnus opus or highest achievement of the powers of darkness.

The diabolical powers and principalities control the illusion or fake reality. (Just like HAL controlled the spaceship) "In Gnosticism, the archons (from Greek *arkhon*, "ruler") were evil, sadistic beings who controlled the earth, as well as many of the thoughts, feelings, and actions of humans. They assisted their master, the demiurge, with the world's creation and continued to help him administer his oppressive rule." (Gnosticism Explained)

They are considered celestial beings and forces of evil. According to Gnostic writings, seven primary archons are associated with the seven planets of the ancient world. They rule the Kingdom of Darkness by preventing souls from leaving the material world.

Is it possible that the gargoyles on buildings represent the demonic spiritual beings who are watching over humanity and keeping individuals trapped in a fake reality or simulation? One can argue that it was the god of this world that hijacked the bishops and Constantine at the Council of Nicaea in 325 A.D. and used the counterfeit spirit to write the Nicene Creed. It was the forces of darkness who took control of the Council and orchestrated the final vote. Constantine and Nicaea's small group of bishops were pawns of the archonic demons.

These demonic powers and rulers are deceivers and liars. Perhaps the archons, used mental telepathy or mind control to manipulate Constantine and the bishops. It makes little difference how they did it, more importantly they were successful. The archons with the help of the small group of bishops and the pagan Emperor Constantine created a counterfeit spirit to control the world. It is manifested in a man-made religious system and a diabolical creed. Billions of unawakened souls worldwide are in bondage to the man-made religion of the archons or evil rulers of this world.

The counterfeit spirit explains the hokus pokus and delusional thinking of man-made religion. It also reveals how the Father of Lies used the counterfeit spirit to transform himself into an angel of light.

And no marvel; for Satan himself is transformed into an angel of light. 2 Cor 11:14

The counterfeit spirit is the cornerstone for man-made religion. It has tricked and deceived humanity for two thousand years. But in vain they do worship me, teaching for doctrines the commandments of men. Matt 15:8

The Synagogue of Satan

The synagogue of Satan appears two times in the book of Revelations. Because this book is filled with symbolism and hidden meanings, it is difficult to understand.   It is unfortunate, but many Bible scholars use these two verses to attack the Jewish people.

I know thy works, and tribulation, and poverty, (but thou art rich) and I know the blasphemy of them which say they are Jews, and are not, but are the *synagogue of Satan.* Rev 2:9

Behold, I will make them of the *synagogue of Satan,* which say they are Jews, and are not, but do lie; behold, I will make them to come and worship before thy feet, and to know that I have loved thee. Rev 3:9

The synagogue of Satan is not a building located in the ancient cities of Smyrna or Philadelphia. The synagogue of Satan is a "prison" inside your mind. The "guards" are the rulers and principalities who keep unawakend souls from knowing the truth. They control beliefs of unawakened souls by perpetuating hokus pokus and delusional thinking. Their job is to keep individuals shackled to the "cave" or the Synagogue of Satan. The "guards or archons are like Agent Smith in the Matrix movie who keep humanity in bondage to the Matrix. When you give permission to the "demons" or archons power to control your thoughts and actions, you agree to stay in the Synagogue of Satan. When fear, guilt, condemnation, materialism, evil, and idolatry exists in your mind, one is "demon possessed" and imprisoned in the *synagogue of Satan.*

One can also call this the carnal mind. "For to be carnally minded is death; but to be spiritually minded is life and peace. Because the *carnal mind is enmity* against God: for it is not subject to the law of God, neither indeed can be. So then they that are in the flesh cannot please God." Rom 8 6-8 The Latin word "enmity" is *inimicus* which means animosity, hatred, or hostility.

It is important to comprehend what this verse is really saying. The carnal mind is *death,* animosity, hatred, and hostility to the True God. One cannot serve two masters.

"No man can serve two masters: for either he will hate the one and love the other; or else he will hold to the one and despise the other. Ye cannot serve God and mammon." Matt 6:24

The definition of mammon from the Dictionary from Oxford Languages is wealth regarded as an evil influence or *false object of worship and devotion.*

Hokus Pokus
A Practical Guide to Deconstruction

Christians cannot worship two masters, the false gods Yahweh and Jesus of Nazareth and the One True God, Abba Father at the same time.

Just like the prisoners in Plato's cave, one must make a life changing decision to leave the "cave" and return to the True God or remain in the cave and believe the shadows on the wall are real.

The Gnostics believed in one supreme, omnipotent, and absolute God who is above everything. They called the supreme God the Monad. "The Monad is a monarchy with nothing above it. It is he who exists as God and Father of everything, the invisible One who is above everything, who exists as incorruption, which is in the pure light into which no eye can look. He is the invisible Spirit, of whom it is not right to think of him as a god, or something similar. For he is more than a god, since there is nothing above him, for no one lords it over him. For he does not exist in something inferior to him since everything exists in him. For it is he who establishes himself. He is eternal since he does not need anything. For he is total perfection. (The Apocryphon of John the Nag Hammadi Library)

The creator God of Judaism, Christianity, and Islam is not the True God. Yahweh is a jealous, tyrannical, cruel, malevolent god who condones genocide, murders, rape, and incest. The Gnostics called this lower god the demiurge or Yaldabaoth.

Jesus of Nazareth, Paul, and the first Christians recognized that Yahweh was not the True God. God the Father in the New Testament was loving and full of mercy. Both Jesus of Nazareth and Gnostic Paul called the True God Abba Father. This is an Aramaic word to address God the Father from a deep and intimate relationship.

For ye have not received the spirit of bondage again to fear; but ye have received the Spirit of adoption, whereby we cry, Abba, Father. Romans 8:15

"*Abba*, Father, "he said, "everything is possible for you. Take this cup from me. Yet not what I will, but what you will." Mark 14:36

Because you are sons, God has sent forth the Spirit of His Son into our hearts, crying, "Abba! Father!" Gal 4:6

Man-made religion hides the truth from unawakened souls

by preaching a false gospel, avoiding any Bible verses that talk about ideas that contradict their hokus pokus. Man-made religion spins the truth, so it agrees with the counterfeit spirit. Christianity dances around the dark side of Yahweh and portrays him as an all loving and merciful God. Although Christianity claims the God revealed in the Old Testament is the same God in the New Testament, this is hokus pokus and delusional thinking perpetuated by the Father of Lies.

- Now therefore *kill every male among the little ones and kill every woman that hath known man by lying with him.* But all the women children, that have not known a man by lying with him, keep alive for yourselves. Num 31 17-18

- Now go and smite Amalek, and utterly *destroy all that they have, and spare them not; but slay both man and woman, infant and suckling, ox and sheep, camel and ass.* 1 Sam 15 2-4

- The LORD regretted that he had made human beings on the earth, and his heart was deeply troubled. So the LORD said, *"I will wipe from the face of the earth the human race I have created*—and with them the animals, the birds and the creatures that move along the ground—for I regret that I have made them. Gen 6:6

Because the Catholic Church labeled the Gnostics heretics, destroyed their literature, and killed thousands of true believers, the world has been kept in the spiritual dark ages for two thousand years. Whenever a truth seeker sees or hears the word "heresy" or "heretic," consider this a spiritual calling to find out why man-made religion wants to hide this information from you. They are the heretics, by their fruits you shall know them.

The study of Gnosticism is a portal into the beliefs of the earliest believers before Constantine. Between 325 A.D and today, humanity has been in the spiritual dark ages. One must study the wisdom of the ancients before Constantine to unlock the truth. Man-made religion is a wolf in sheep's clothing trying to hide the truth and keep humanity away from knowing the True God and returning to our spiritual home.

The Apostles Creed should be renamed the Creed of the Satan because it is diabolical and blasphemes the True God. It is a creed of lies, deceptions, and delusional thinking that keeps unawakened souls in bondage to the archon rulers of this world.

Their creed shackles unawakened souls like the prisoners in the cave and tricks them to believe the shadows are real. In modern society both Catholics and Protestants fundamentally agree with the Nicene Creed. They are both in a strong delusion and believe a lie.

Hokus Pokus
A Practical Guide to Deconstruction

The Nicene Creed is a doctrine of the Satan because it makes Jesus of Nazareth equal to the True God. The archons are deceivers and thrive on telling lies. They use the counterfeit spirit to conceal the truth and keep unawakened souls trapped in the man-made religion of the archons.

Jesus of Nazareth never said he was God, equal to the Father. The demonic forces at the Council of Nicaea in 325 A.D. created a delusion and a blasphemous lie. It was their diabolical goal to maintain control of unawakened souls and keep them separated from the True God.

Man-made religion is a "shadow" perpetuated by the counterfeit spirit. Plato's Allegory of the Cave is a fitting reminder about the prisoners who chose to remain in the cave believing the shadows were real.

This is disturbing material but necessary information for anyone who wants to leave the cave. This book has discussed several important topics that expose the hokus pokus in man-made religion. If the reader takes the "red pill," there will be a compelling desire to check this out for yourself until you find what you are seeking. When you find it, The Truth will set you free.

Jesus said, "Let one who seeks *not stop seeking until that person finds*; and upon finding, *the person will be disturbed*; and being disturbed, will be astounded; and will reign over the entirety."

Gospel of Thomas Saying 2

One Nation Under God

It is necessary to review some important information previously discussed in this book to prepare the reader for this disturbing content. The Ancient Gnostics, Cathars, and other dualistic traditions believed the Demiurge or Satan is the god of this world. Because the Catholic Church did not want this knowledge revealed to the public, these believers were labeled heretics. Thousands of innocent souls were tortured and burned at the stake. Thousands of scared scrolls kept in the Great Library of Alexandria were burned by Roman Catholics. This is an important question, what was the Catholic Church hiding? The Age of Aquarius is tearing down the curtain of hokus pokus and delusional thinking, revealing truths that have been hidden and covered up for two thousand years.

Satan rules over every aspect of our society, i.e., government, education, religion, banking, military, corporations, and social media, etc. He has blinded the minds of both individuals and nations to keep humanity ignorant from knowing the glorious gospel of the Christ within who is the image of the true God.

The demiurge or Satan is the god of this world. "In whom *the god of this world hath blinded the minds of them which believe not,* lest the light of the glorious gospel of Christ, who is the image of God, should shine unto them." 2 Cor 4:4 The god of this world is the "Lord" in the Old Testament, Yahweh.

Satan appears as an angel of light. (2 Cor 11:14) He has hijacked the minds and souls of mankind into believing a gigantic lie. Because Satan has exalted himself as the true god through the counterfeit spirit, unawakened souls unknowingly worship the demiurge or the god of this world rather than the True God.

Skeptics and Christian apologists (archonic thinking) will argue this idea as foolish thinking and heretical. They are really defending the "god of this world" who is determined to keep unawakened souls shackled to the shadows of hokus pokus and delusional thinking. Truth-seekers will discover that the concept of dualism, a lower god and True God, goes back to Plato thousands of years ago. Gnostic Paul's epistles are filled with ancient ideas about dualism that the modern world does not understand. He wrote about the god of this world and powers and principalities from a Gnostic perspective.

Satan shackles humanity to a man-made religious system that exalts the false god, Yahweh. This book previously discussed how Yahweh was transformed from a lower, warrior, and tribal god into God Almighty. Both Judaism and Christianity recognize Yahweh as God. The counterfeit spirit tricks unawakened souls into believing they are worshiping God while they actually worship Yahweh, the god of this world.

Although this sounds like heresy, the Christian Bible says this over and over again for those with ears to hear.

The counterfeit spirit infiltrates all aspects of society. The collective unconsciousness of our nation has been tricked into believing that we are a Christian nation under God. Because most Americans believe the evil, tyrannical god of the Old Testament is the True God, our nation unknowingly prays to the devil or the god of this world. This collective agreement "makes a deal with the devil" and sells out the soul of our nation to the god of this world.

Earlier in this book, the section "Reinventing God" revealed there are two distinct Gods in the Bible. The Old Testament God who is evil, malevolent psychopath who kills men, women, children, and animals. There is also a loving Father that Jesus of Nazareth and Gnostic Paul called Abba Father. Because Christians embrace the idea that the evil God of the Old Testament and loving God of the New Testament are the same, there is a collective agreement that Yahweh is the True God.

One can learn more about this topic on YouTube.

Did Jesus Worship Yahweh by Paul Wallis
https://youtu.be/WZg6_eqczMI

Early Christians: Yahweh is actually the Devil, an interview with M. David Litwa,   https://youtu.be/6t3neg3J7gY

Jesus of Nazareth did not worship or pray to Yahweh. He rebuked the Jewish religious leaders because they believed Yahweh was the True God. "Ye are of *your father the devil*, and the lusts of your father ye will do. He was a murderer from the beginning, and abode not in the truth, because there is no truth in him. When he speaketh a lie, he speaketh of his own: for he is a liar, and the father of it." John 8:44 Some scholars point out the Greek translation says, "You are from the father of the devil."

The father of the devil is Yahweh.

Hokus Pokus
A Practical Guide to Deconstruction

Jesus of Nazareth was sent to reveal this important truth to humanity, Yahweh is a liar and the father of lies. He is the god of this world and the power of darkness. Jesus of Nazareth taught his disciples about the True God. "If ye had known me, ye should have known my Father also: and from henceforth ye know him and have seen him." John 14:7

The idea that Yahweh is the True God is hokus pokus. Jesus of Nazareth revealed the True God when He spoke about his Father in heaven. He called him Father, our Father, and Abba Father. Christians who worship Yahweh as their true God, are embracing the demiurge, or the ruler of this world who is Satan.

When Jesus of Nazareth rebuked the Pharisees, he was speaking to everyone who believes Yahweh is the True God. This includes individuals, man-made religions, and nations.

The United States has a Pledge of Allegiance that we memorized as children. In 1954, President Eisenhower asked Congress to add the words "under God." So now it reads...

"I pledge allegiance to the flag of the United States of America, and to the republic for which it stands, *one nation under God*, indivisible, with liberty and justice for all."

In the context of what you just read, who is "God" in the Pledge of Allegiance? Is the United States one nation under the Judeo-Christian God, Yahweh?

Millions of patriotic Americans who recite the Pledge of Allegiance are unknowingly pledging allegiance to the evil and malevolent demiurge or the devil? This collective agreement by millions of Americans empowers Satan to manifest more chaos, evil, and suffering on our nation and its citizens.

Jesus of Nazareth was also pointing his finger at the United States when He said *"Ye are of your father the devil*, and the lusts of your father ye will do. He was a murderer from the beginning, and abode not in the truth, because there is no truth in him. When he speaketh a lie, he speaketh of his own: for he is a liar, and the father of it. John 8"44

Is America one nation under God? If it is, then one needs to ask why are there so many pagan images in our nation's capital? This is a similar question that was asked previously in this book... Why are there so many gargoyles roosting on churches and cathedrals?

Hokus Pokus
A Practical Guide to Deconstruction

On top of the United States Capitol is the Statue of Freedom. A picture is worth a thousand words because the Statue of Freedom is the Greek goddess, Athena. Other pagan deities are also mentioned. Libertas is the Roman goddess and personification of liberty. Libertas is associated with Ishtar who has many attributes including the goddess of war. In Homer's Iliad, Athena was a war goddess and is synonymous with military prowess. The statue of Athena is a gigantic bronze figure that stands 19 ½ feet tall and weighs approximately 15,000 pounds. "She is an allegorical figure whose right hand holds the hilt of a sheathed sword, while a laurel wreath of victory and the Shield of the United States are clasped in her left hand. Her chiton is secured by a brooch inscribed "U.S." and is partially covered by a heavy, Native American–style fringed blanket thrown over her left shoulder. She faces east toward the main entrance of the building and the rising Sun. She wears a military helmet adorned with stars and an eagle's head which is itself crowned by an umbrella-like crest of feathers." (Wikipedia)

There are many pagan images and symbols in prominent view throughout our nation's capital. The George Washington Monument is designed after a pagan Egyptian obelisk. In Egyptian mythology, the obelisk symbolized the sun god Ra. The Apotheosis of Washington inside the rotunda of the capitol pictures George

Washing ascending as a god. Several of the famous buildings and monuments resemble Greek temples; for example, the Supreme Court Building, the Lincoln Memorial, and even the Capitol Building have features that resemble ancient Greek temples.

One of the largest and most famous monuments in the United States is the Statue of Liberty that portrays a pagan goddess watching over New York Harbor. It serves as a demonic idol paying homage to the powers of darkness who rule over this nation.

Although our currency says, "In God We Trust." It has cryptic images of the all-seeing eye, a pyramid separated in two parts, and the Latin words "annuit coeptis" and "novus ordo seclorum." Several U.S. coins have both the words "In God We Trust" and the imprint of the pagan goddess Libertas.

If the United States is one nation under the True God, there should be visible evidence of peace, harmony, love, and brotherhood. On the other hand, if the United States is "one nation under the evil lower god, the demiurge or Satan," there should be evidence of war, slavery, abortion, corruption, servitude, hatred, bigotry, etc.

The United States has been in twelve major wars that have killed over one million patriotic Americans. It is estimated that there were approximately ten million slaves between 1619 and 1865.

Millions of babies are aborted every year. The United States military spending accounts for 12 percent of the federal budget. Military spending is the highest in the world and overshadows all other countries. There is an epidemic of drug addictions, mental health disorders, and murders. Currently the United States is at its highest rate of imprisonment in history.

Is this what it means to be "one nation under God?" Which God are Americans pledging allegiance to?

America is under Yahweh.

The father of the devil is Yahweh.

Closing Thoughts

True or False

This is a true or false question and one of the most important questions a person can ask themselves. Please check your correct answer.

______ Jesus of Nazareth is the Son of God, equal to the Father, coeternal, having one substance and essence.

______ Jesus of Nazareth is a holy man, prophet, a created being, not equal to the Father.

______ Not sure, I need more information.

Although Christians will check the first box, Jews, Muslims, Hindus, and Buddhists will mark the second box. Regardless of one's faith, everyone believes their answer is correct.

Individuals who are deconstructing their faith use critical thinking to fact check their core beliefs. Truth seekers are asking themselves extremely difficult questions and rethinking many of their core beliefs, that they inherited from their parents.

Modern Day Idolatry

Eventually, every truth seeker must reach a conclusion about Jesus of Nazareth. Was He God in the flesh or just a holy man who attained Christ Consciousness? Should you trust Constantine and the small group of bishops at the Council of Nicaea who voted to make Jesus of Nazareth the Son of God in the flesh the source of your belief? Should you trust the man-made religion (know them by their fruits) who tells the world that the man, Jesus of Nazareth, is God and equal to the True God? More importantly, can you trust yourself to make this weighty decision without taking the time to acquire knowledge and gnosis from outside sources? Because this book raises many questions about the hokus pokus that undermines the integrity and honesty of the Roman Church, you are now better prepared to make an informed decision about the divinity of Jesus.

If Jesus of Nazareth is <u>not</u> the Son of God in the flesh, then devout Christians are unknowingly committing idolatry. "Therefore watch yourselves very carefully, so that you do not become corrupt and make for yourselves an idol, an image of any shape, whether formed *like a man* or a woman, or like any animal on earth or any bird that flies in the air, or like any creature that moves along the ground or any fish in the waters below." Deut 4 15-18 An idol is anything that replaces or comes before the one, True God.

Jesus of Nazareth never claimed to be the Son of God, equal to the True God; nor did he ask his disciples to worship him.

- "And for this cause God shall send them strong delusion, that they should believe a lie: That they all might be damned who believed not the truth but had pleasure in unrighteousness. 2 Thes 2 11-12

- "I can of mine own self do nothing: as I hear, I judge and my judgment is just; because I seek not mine own will, but the will of the Father which hath sent me." John 5:30

- "Jesus said, "The Father is greater than I." John 14:28

- "Why do you call me good?" Jesus answered. "No one is good—except God alone. Mark 10:18

- "Verily, verily, I say unto you, He that believeth on me, the works that I do shall he do also; and greater works than these shall he do; because I go unto my Father." John 14:12

- "And they were offended in him. But Jesus said unto them, A prophet is not without honour, save in his own country, and in his own house." Matt 13:57

- "For I have not spoken of myself, but the Father who sent me, he gave me a commandment, what I should say and what I should speak." John 12:49 (The KJB does not capitalize myself or me.)

- "Ye men of Israel, hear these words; Jesus of Nazareth, a man approved of God among you by miracles and wonders and signs, which God did by him in the midst of you, as ye yourselves also know." Acts 2:22

- But now ye seek to kill me, <u>a man</u> that hath told you the truth, which I have heard of God: this did not Abraham. Ye do the deeds of your father. Then said they to him, We be not born of fornication; we have one Father, even God. John 8:40-41

The material in this book is only the tip of the iceberg. I hope you will take the time to check out the information that you just read and expand it further by studying what other truth seekers have to say.

To Be Continued…

In the beginning of the book there is a quote from Socrates. I will end the book with the same quote.

Socrates said,

"I cannot teach anybody anything.

I can only make them think."

Thank you for reading my book.
Best wishes on your journey along the "yellow brick road."

Francis Marion

Contact Information:

hokuspokus.info

francismarion@hokuspokus.info

About the Author

Francis Marion is not a scholar or theologian. He is just a regular guy who took the "red pill" (in the Matrix movie) about twenty years ago. He was a prisoner in a dark spiritual cave who chose to escape. The climb out of the cave required hours of research, study, and contemplation. The ascent out of the cave was difficult and disturbing. It required him to deprogram his mind and toss out everything that he believed. He eventually learned that the shadows in his cave were not real, and all the people who taught him about God, as a child and later as an adult, were not telling the truth. He recognized the brilliant light at the opening of the cave as the True God and everything else were just shadows.